love guitar

© Andy Read 2(
loveguitar.co.uk

The right of Andy Read to be identified as the author of this work has been asserted in accordance with the copyright, designs and patents act 1988.

All rights reserved.
No part of this publication may be reproduced, stored in a retrieval system, used to light a fire, kill a spider, or transmitted in any form or by any means, electronic, mechanical, photocopying, recording, or otherwise, without the prior permission of the publisher.

This guitar tuition method © Andy Read 2009/2011/2016
Designed on a Mac using Comic Life 3
Cover by Dave House (noahsart.co.uk)
Front cover photo by Jaz Read

500 limited edition print run
Meticulously printed and bound
c/o Stephen Edwards @ Culverlands in Winchester, UK
Calibri 9pt for main text

Big thanks for extra mile help:
Jemima Lewis
Dave House
Mark Irving
Jane Read
Mark Lewis (pre-press king)
Mark Pearson (Comic Life/Plasq)

firsthouse publishing

I have had holidays in
London ○ Paris ○ Madrid ○ New York

Introduction

Want to learn guitar? You've come to the right place!

But where do you start? How do you begin?

1. Get a guitar:
Try and get yourself a classical nylon string. They are cheap to buy, and easy on your fingers compared to steel strings. The neck is also quite wide, giving your fingers a little more room to learn the chord shapes. A ¾ size guitar will usually be fine for most primary school age children – but I do know some 10 year olds happy with a full size! Walk into any guitar shop and try out both. You'll get either for under £80 new, and much less second hand.

2. Make sure it's in tune:
For now, ask a more experienced musician to tune it for you. Sometimes strings detune a little just with damp and humidity around the house, so get yourself a decent £15 electronic tuner, or a free smart phone app to help you make those minor adjustments. There's also a detailed manual method of tuning at the back of this book.

3. Start playing:
Whether you are playing single note TAB, or strumming chords; the point is you are introducing your fingertips to something they have not experienced before. Don't worry if they feel a little sore when you start playing, this is very normal. As your fingertips toughen up the pain will disappear after a few weeks of playing regularly.

4. Keep playing:
Remember when you started to ride a bike, or stepped on a skateboard for the first time? It felt strange and may have taken a little while to get used to, but if you persevered and kept getting on that bike, and hopping on that skateboard you improved, right? That is exactly the same for your guitar. The more time you put into it, the better you will become!

Contents

Chapter 1: The Ten Basics

Guitar parts – Finger names – Open string names – The left hand home position – The chord box – Six must-know chords – TAB – The rest stroke (right hand) – Finger picking (right hand) –   Strumming (right hand) – Tuning.

5

Chapter 2: How to Play TAB

TAB intro – "Ten Green Bottles" – "Happy Birthday" – "Old Macdonald" – "Jingle Bells" – "Merry Christmas" – "Oh When the Saints" – The blues scale – "The Grand Old Duke of York" – The G major scale.

19

Chapter 3: How to Play Chords

Chords intro – Learning the chords of E, A, B7, D, G, C, (including easy versions) – Learning to change quickly and in time between chords – The 16 chord block exercise – Learning how to strum – The 4 basic strumming patterns.

33

Chapter 4: How to Finger Pick

Finger picking intro – Finger names (right hand) – Finger picking three strings – Finger picking 6 strings – using the 16 chord block progression to develop moving from one chord to another quickly and in time – The 4 basic finger picking patterns.

47

Chapter 5: Understanding Classical Notation

Rest stroke – Crotchet and minims – Dotted minims and semibreves – The stave – The notes of E, B, G, F, C, D, and various songs using these notes – G and C major scale.

61

Chapter 6: Back of the Book Extras

Scales – Half-bar/full-bar chords – Minor chords – Ten cool riffs – Ten cool chord progressions – "Minuet in G" – "Greensleeves" TAB – Ten songs using three chords – Really useful chord page.

83

Watch the videos
www.loveguitar.co.uk

Videos of every page including songs, chords and riffs are on the website – useful to watch and see how they're played, and helpful to listen to hear how they sound.

Self evaluation progress squares

Beside each song or lesson there are squares for you to fill in as you go. It's a really helpful way of seeing how well you think you're getting on, and how much you think you have achieved so far.

The five squares are for songs, and the three squares are for lessons.

(for songs)

☑ (played through once)
☑ ☑ (played through 5 times)
☑ ☑ ☑ (partly off by heart)
☑ ☑ ☑ ☑ (fully off by heart)
☑ ☑ ☑ ☑ ☑ (eyes closed)

(for lessons)

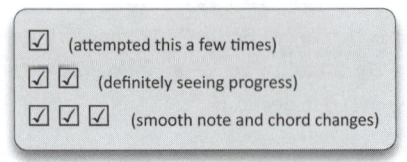

☑ (attempted this a few times)
☑ ☑ (definitely seeing progress)
☑ ☑ ☑ (smooth note and chord changes)

Have you ever played in a sports team with a coach? (I don't mean the ones that transport you to away matches) They are the people who run the team on the training pitch. Bad coaches push too hard and make you feel bad, while good coaches are encouraging and inspire you to improve. Try and be a helpful coach to yourself. Rather than being quick to see how slow you think you may be progressing, try and think of the things you **are** getting better at. Remember, if you pick up your guitar regularly enough **you will improve**; but for your own encouragement it's important **you** see your own progress – and that your hard work is paying off!

For parents/carers;

What this book is all about...

Primary beginners only need just enough information to move ahead one step at a time. When you start running you don't really need to worry about expensive trainers, a strict diet, or know 101 important techniques. You're just looking for a helpful easy-to-understand exercise plan for the first few weeks and months – a simple method that gradually eases you in gently with the goal of being able to put one foot in front of the other for 30 minutes without stopping! If you enjoy that and want to be more committed you will naturally want to explore further technical aspects in order to improve along the way.
This book is concerned with that first part of the journey. I've concentrated on giving students just what they need as a beginner and purposefully left it uncluttered with more complex skills and concepts easily learnt at a later stage. To truly learn and understand anything it's healthy and wise to have a few information sources. I hope that this particular method, alongside others, will help the beginner to reach the ultimate guitarist's goal; to play, to progress, to enjoy!

1 The Ten Basics

This first chapter is like a quick start guide; ten simple things you need to know right at the beginning of your journey. In the chapters following we'll be jumping further into the deep end but for now, take as much time as you need to get familiar with the basics.

Page

Basics lesson 1: Guitar parts 6

Basics lesson 2: Finger names – Open string names 7

Basics lesson 3: The left hand home position 8

Basics lesson 4: The chord box 9

Basics lesson 5: Six must-know chords 10

Basics lesson 6: TAB 11

Basics lesson 7: The rest stroke (right hand) 12

Basics lesson 8: Finger picking (right hand) 13

Basics lesson 9: Strumming (right hand) 14

Basics lesson 10: Tuning 16

Basics lesson 1: Guitar parts

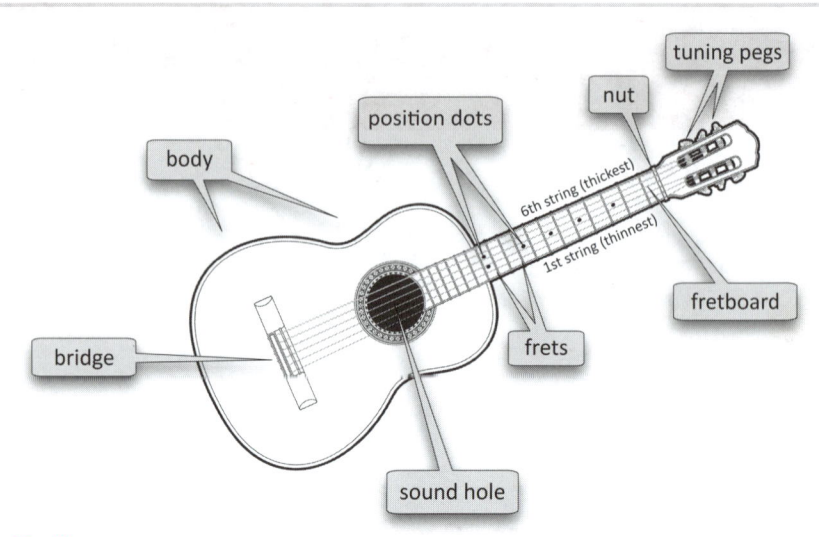

Labels on guitar diagram: tuning pegs, nut, position dots, body, 6th string (thickest), 1st string (thinnest), fretboard, bridge, frets, sound hole

Body: The main hollow part of the guitar that gives the notes the depth of sound when the strings are played.

Position dots: These are like road signs for the fingers to help you remember where they are on the fretboard. Most guitars have them on the 3rd, 5th, 7th, 9th, and 12th fret.

Nut: The bar of white plastic between the head and the fretboard that holds and supports the strings in place.

Tuning pegs: These tighten or loosen the strings – this changes the pitch, and are how each string is tuned correctly to each other.

Fretboard: (fingerboard) The top strip of wood on the neck of the guitar that the frets lie across. The strings run over the fretboard between the nut and bridge.

Frets: The metal strips that lie across the fretboard.

Sound hole: This helps to project the sound of the chords or notes when the strings are played.

Bridge: This supports the strings coming from the nut and fixes them to the top of the body (sometimes called a sound board).

Basics lesson 2: Finger names

```
       middle
index   m    ring         Middle
  i          r           Ring  M  Index
             Little       R        I
             L                        Thumb
                                        T

   Left hand              Right hand
  (fretboard)           (finger picking)
```

Open string names

Open strings are just the strings plucked on their own without using any fretboard fingers.

This is a simple phrase to help you remember – always start from the 1st string (thinnest).

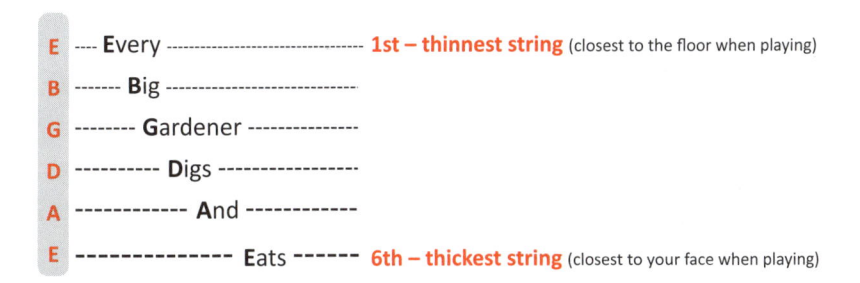

E ---- **E**very -------------------------------- **1st – thinnest string** (closest to the floor when playing)

B ------- **B**ig ----------------------------

G -------- **G**ardener ----------------

D ---------- **D**igs -----------------

A ------------ **A**nd ------------

E -------------- **E**ats ------ **6th – thickest string** (closest to your face when playing)

Another helpful way of orientating the guitar strings with the six lines on the page is to lay the guitar flat on your knees (strings on top) with the book opened flat on a table right in front of you. This way, the six lines correspond exactly to the six guitar strings, and are directly parallel.

> **Top Tip** *As students progress (in the classical style especially) they will learn the technical names referring to the left hand fingers as 1,2,3,4 (index, middle, ring, Little) and the right hand fingers with the Spanish names P, I, M, A (Pulgar/Thumb, Indice/Index, Medio/Middle, Anular/Ring).

Basics lesson 3: The left hand home position

Try to get your left hand to look like this;

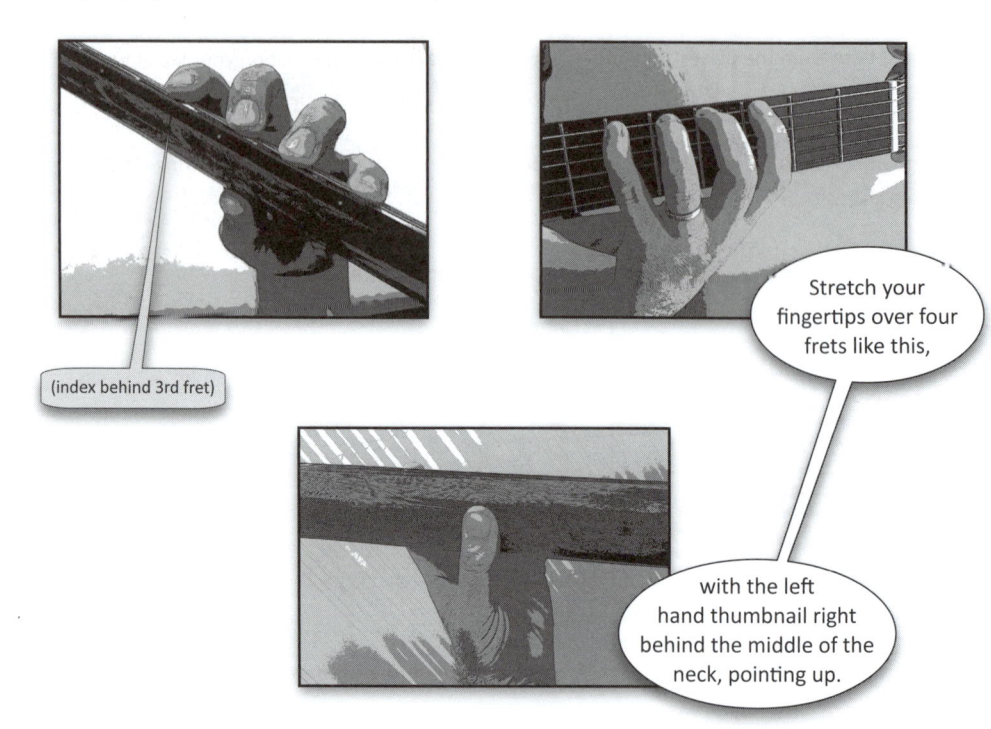

(index behind 3rd fret)

Stretch your fingertips over four frets like this,

with the left hand thumbnail right behind the middle of the neck, pointing up.

Thumb: place it behind the 4th fret with the nail half way down, pointing up.
Fingertips: place the index, middle, ring, and little fingers on the thickest string (6th) just behind the 3rd, 4th, 5th, and 6th frets. Create an arch or bridge so that your fingers do not come into contact with any other strings.
Wrist: push it slightly forward.

Remember these shapes; a good home position technique will make sure your fingers reach easily over the strings to the right place on the fretboard.

Your thumb behind the neck will act like a clamp and help you press the fingertips down firmly. This will help to get the best sounding notes without any muffles or buzzing!

> **Top Tip** The first few times you attempt this it maybe a little painful, but after regular practice your muscles will begin to co-operate!

Basics lesson 4: The chord box

This is how you read a chord box.

It is set out from the player's point of view, so if you lay your guitar flat on your lap, it will be very similar.

Remember; with the guitar in the playing position on your thigh, the thickest string (6th) is closest to your face.

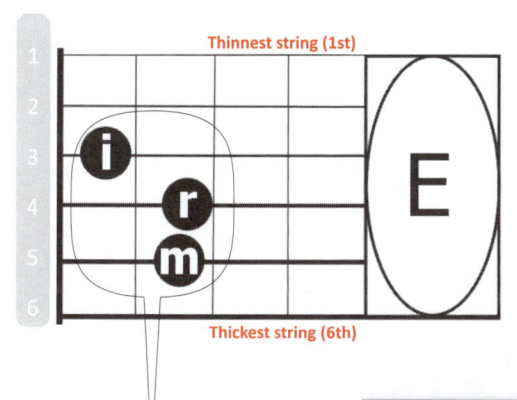

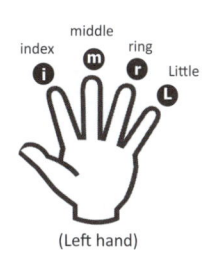

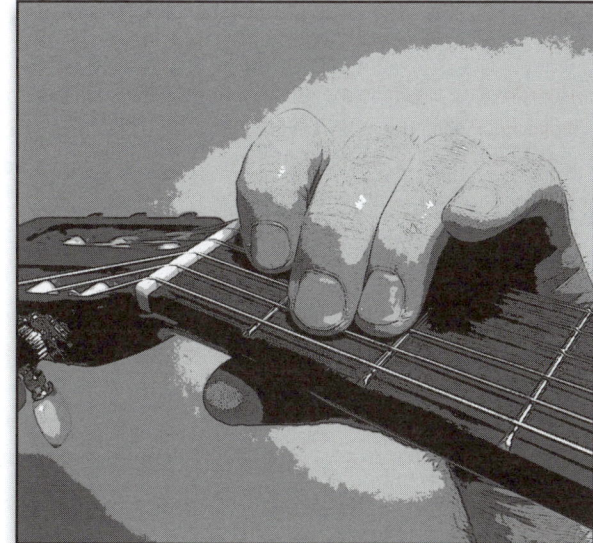

Basics lesson 5: Six must-know chords

Easy versions of the chords are perfect for young beginners.

Down strum each chord X4 using your RH thumb.

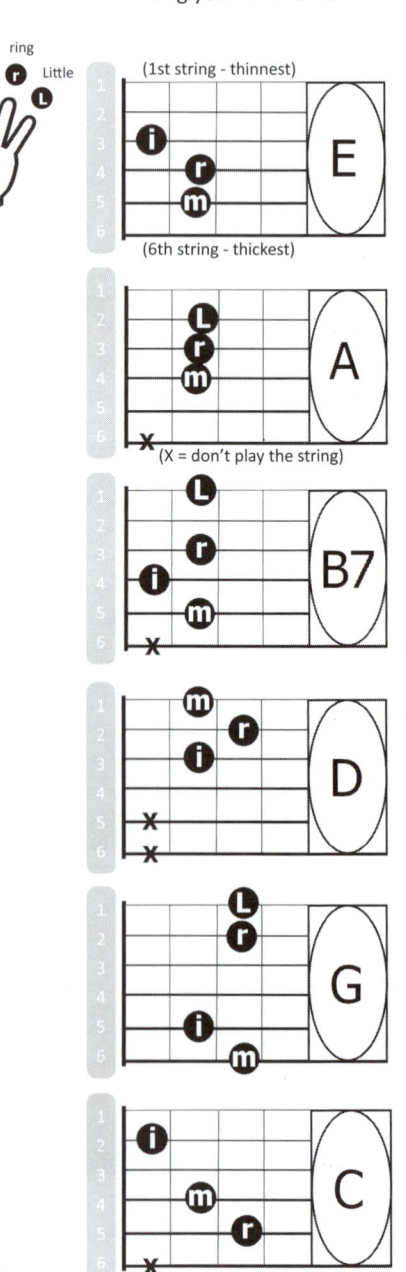

(X = don't play the string)

(1st string - thinnest)
(6th string - thickest)

(X = don't play the string)

Basics lesson 6: TAB (guitar tablature)

TAB is short for guitar tablature, and is a form of notation that uses lines (representing the strings) and numbers (fret numbers) to show you where to place your fingers on the fretboard. TAB is a quick and easy way to play tunes using single notes.

There are three things to remember with TAB:

The six lines represent the six strings

The top line is always the thinnest string (1st)
(closest to the floor when playing)

The numbers show you which fret to place your fingertips on

The pictures explain the diagram.

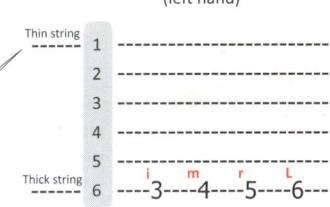

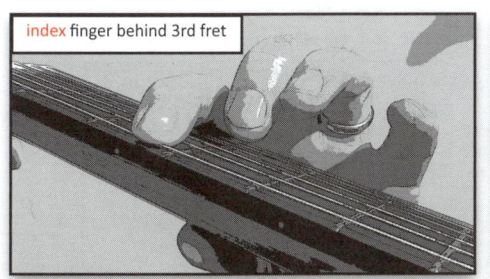

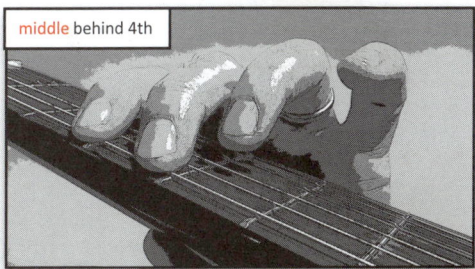

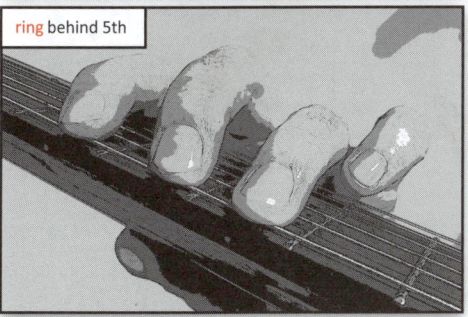

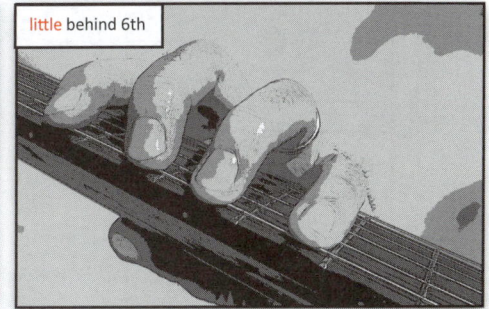

index finger behind 3rd fret

middle behind 4th

ring behind 5th

little behind 6th

Basics lesson 7: The rest stroke (right hand)

The rest stroke is a technique that is used to play single notes in TAB/classical notation (Chapter 5). It's also the easiest way to produce the clearest sounding note.

It gets its name because after plucking the string, the finger rests on the adjacent string after it follows through, giving a slightly rounder, often punchier sound.

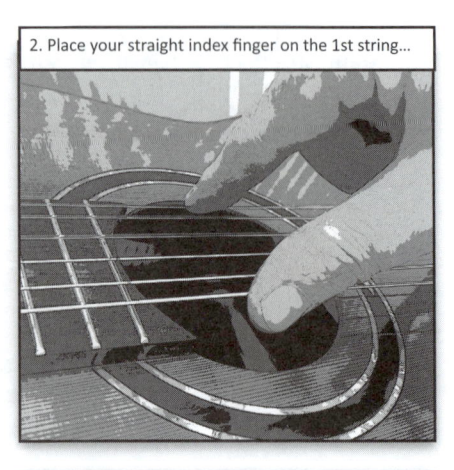

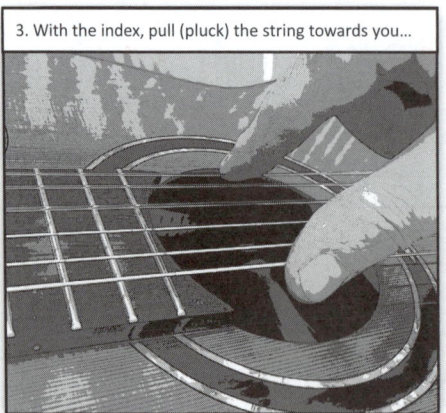

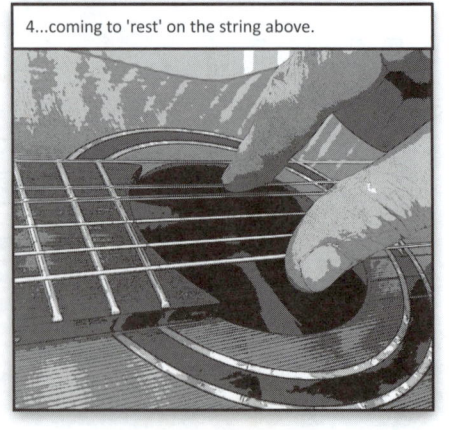

1. Place your right hand thumb on the top string (6th)...

2. Place your straight index finger on the 1st string...

3. With the index, pull (pluck) the string towards you...

4. ...coming to 'rest' on the string above.

Top Tip — For simplicity this technique can be used by the RH index finger on the 1st, 2nd, and 3rd string, while the RH thumb uses it when playing notes on the 6th, 5th, or 4th string. With the thumb you simply press/pluck down on the string away from you, and come to 'rest' on the string below.

Basics lesson 8: Finger picking (right hand)

Finger picking is a technique that uses the fingertips to pluck individual strings. It's mainly used with chords (played by the left hand), and unique as it adds a variety of sounds by picking out the different notes of that chord.

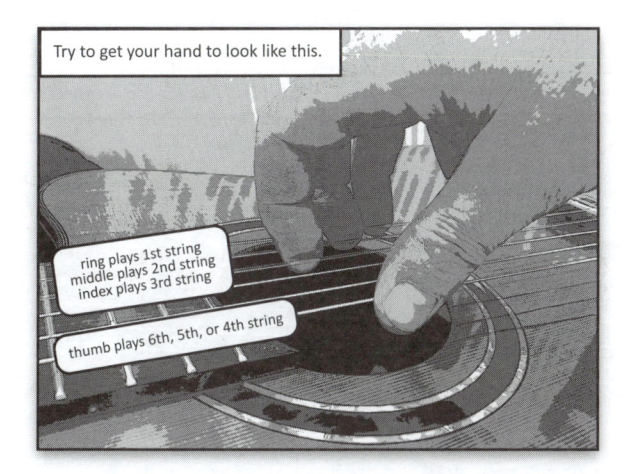

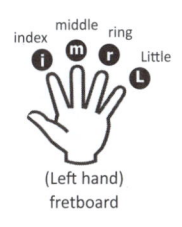

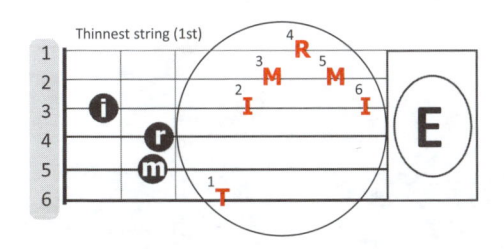

Try to get your hand to look like this.

ring plays 1st string
middle plays 2nd string
index plays 3rd string

thumb plays 6th, 5th, or 4th string

(Left hand) fretboard

Thinnest string (1st)

(Right hand) finger picking

Play this basic finger picking pattern using the chord of E. Each finger is assigned to a string. Play the sequence twice, slowly and carefully, starting with the thumb.

Pluck each string in this order: **T, I, M, R, M, I**

Repeat the sequence until it sounds smooth and clean.

Basics lesson 9: Strumming (right hand)

Strumming is the swinging action of the arm with a pick (or thumb) brushing over the strings. It is used when playing chords only, and provides rhythm.

Picks (sometimes called plectrums) come in a variety of thicknesses and colours. Having used many over the years, I really like the Jim Dunlop Nylon .6 or .46.
Players use a pick (as opposed to a thumb) to give a louder and more even strum across the strings.

Hold the pick between your thumb and index finger...

with the pick pointing towards you like this.

The basic strumming pattern
Always start with a down strum...

1 and 2 and 3 and 4 and

1 2 3 4 = down strums

and = up strums

Basics **Ch1 B9**

1

With your left hand playing the E chord, rest the inside of your elbow on the outside edge of the guitar body...

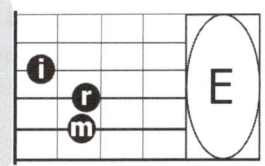

2

then lightly brush the pick (or thumb) downwards across all of the strings...

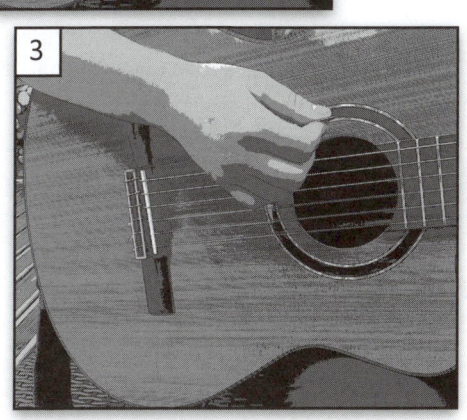

3

and then swing your arm back again brushing the pick (or thumb) over the strings, upwards.

E

Top Tip — Don't worry, it will feel a little awkward and choppy at first, but keep strumming down and up and it will get smoother and cleaner. Swing your arm from your elbow, like a clock pendulum – and try not to twist your wrist. It really is a case of just doing it every day regardless of what it sounds like at the start. Ten minutes a day and I promise you will see a huge difference in a month.

Watch the videos
www.loveguitar.co.uk

Basics lesson 10: Tuning

The easiest and quickest way to tune a guitar is by using a **digital tuner**. A Korg clip-on tuner works great, or try any of the excellent free smart phone apps.

Below is a useful step by step method for tuning your guitar **manually**. Learning this way takes time, so be patient!

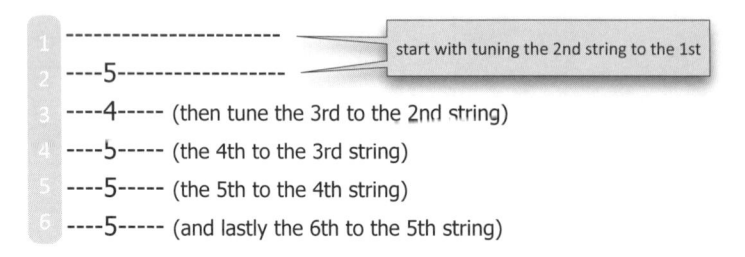

```
1  ----------------------
2  ----5------------------        start with tuning the 2nd string to the 1st
3  ----4----- (then tune the 3rd to the 2nd string)
4  ----5----- (the 4th to the 3rd string)
5  ----5----- (the 5th to the 4th string)
6  ----5----- (and lastly the 6th to the 5th string)
```

1. Place your left hand index finger behind the 5th fret, 2nd string.

2. Pluck the open 1st string, followed by the 2nd string.

3. Listen carefully to the 2nd note (2nd string).

4. Ask yourself, is this 2nd note sound higher or lower than the first note?

If you think this note is higher (sharp), go to the 2nd string's tuning peg ready to turn it. Play the open 2nd string again (take your index finger off) and very slowly turn the peg anti-clockwise to slacken the string – this lowers the pitch of that string's note.
If you think this note is lower (flat), gently turn the tuning peg clockwise to tighten the string. This raises the pitch of that string's note.

5. The goal is to try and get the 2 strings to sound exactly the same (with the 1st open, and 2nd string with the index on 5th fret). If you think they are close, just pluck them both together with your index finger still pressed down on the 5th fret, 2nd string. If they are still out of tune you will hear a wobble or pulsing in the sound. If it is in tune there will be a distinct clean sounding note, ringing true and even.

Now repeat the whole process again, tuning the 3rd string to the 2nd, but this time putting your index finger on the 4th fret. Continue this process until all strings are tuned. This will take time! As you keep practising this your ears will sharpen, your listening will improve, and you will get better and quicker.

The digital method is great if the strings are a little out of tune due to natural humidity changes. If a curious child has been left alone with the tuning pegs however, you might need some help from a more experienced musician to retune!

The manual method is great if you are playing on your own. If you play with others you'll need a reference note to make sure everybody is in tune. This is where the digital tuner is useful because it will give you concert pitch, a standard tuning system that everyone uses worldwide.

> **Top Tip** Learn to listen. This exercise is as much about listening as getting the strings in tune with each other. We start by getting the 2nd string in tune with the 1st. Take time in getting this string in tune – only then move on to tuning the 3rd to the 2nd, and so on.

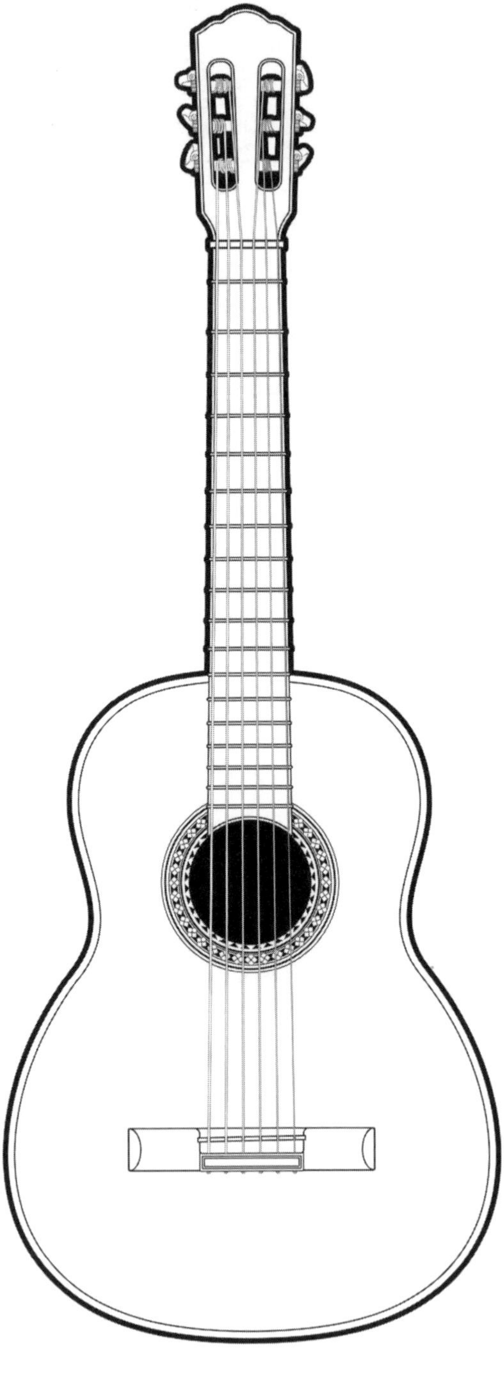

2 How to Play TAB

In this 2nd chapter we shall be learning how to play guitar TAB.

TAB is short for 'guitar tablature', and is a form of notation that uses lines (representing the strings) and numbers (fret numbers) to show you where to place your fingers on the fretboard. It is the easiest and quickest way to start learning songs on the guitar.

TAB shows you what notes to play, but does not indicate rhythm or timing – that's why it really helps to know how the song sounds before you try and learn it. Although classical notation (Chapter 5) does indicate rhythm and timing, it takes more concentration to learn and understand. TAB is quick to grasp and can have you up and running with well known tunes in a very short space of time.

Page

TAB lesson 1: "Easy Peasy", "Lift Off", "Ten Green Bottles" (pt 1) 21

TAB lesson 2: "Jingle Bells" (pt 1), "Old MacDonald", "Happy B'day" (pt 1) 22

TAB lesson 3: "Merry Christmas", "Oh When the Saints", "Happy B'day" (pt 2) ... 23

TAB lesson 4: "Ten Green Bottles" (pt 2), "Jingle Bells" (pt 2), "Swing Low" (pt 1) ... 24

TAB lesson 5: "Oh When the Saints" (full), "Merry Christmas" (pt 2) 25

TAB lesson 6: "10 Green Bottles" (full), Blues Scale in G, "Duke of York" 26

TAB lesson 7: "Blues Solo" (pt 1), "Blues Solo Bass" (pt 1), "Give Me Oil" (pt 1) ... 27

TAB lesson 8: "Blues Solo" (full), "Blues Solo Bass" (full), "Auld Lang Syne" 28

TAB lesson 9: "Merry Christmas" (full), "Give Me Oil In My Lamp" (full) 29

TAB lesson 10: G Major Scale, "Yankee Doodle" 30

TAB intro

The best way to progress is to find out the lesson level you are currently at, then work towards the next lesson. Set yourself a high enough standard to practise the pieces so you can play them confidently and easily with a consistent flow and rhythm.

Use the BSR technique (Bite Size Repetition): take a small section and repeat until you feel there is real improvement. Then take the next short phrase and do the same. Add these two sections together, and as you work through the whole song in this way you will begin to see real progress bit by bit. It's the same principle as polishing a car or your shoes; going over and over, round and round, until it shines.

Under each song there are five self-evaluation squares that help you chart your own progress.

☐ ☐ ☐ ☐ ☐

☑ (played through once)
☑ ☑ (played through 5 times)
☑ ☑ ☑ (partly off by heart)
☑ ☑ ☑ ☑ (fully off by heart)
☑ ☑ ☑ ☑ ☑ (eyes closed) — *This is when you really know a song well!*

As you work on each song, the process and skills acquired to learn it well will help you enormously with learning other songs easier and quicker.

> **Top Tip**
>
> Remember, it's all about good technique.
> Try and get these two good habits into your playing as early as possible:
> **1. Thumb behind the neck/fretboard** – this will help you reach the right notes easily with your fingers.
> **2. Fingertips pressing down, just behind the fret** – this will help you play a good clean note with the least amount of buzzing or muffling.

TAB lesson 1

Work at being confident with two out of the three pieces on every page before moving on to the next lesson – you can use your left hand index or middle finger to play the notes for this lesson. (For the right hand, pluck with your index finger using the rest stroke technique – p12. Also when you see a zero or nought ('0'), it means play the open string i.e. just the string on its own so no left hand fingers needed!).

1. "Easy Peasy"

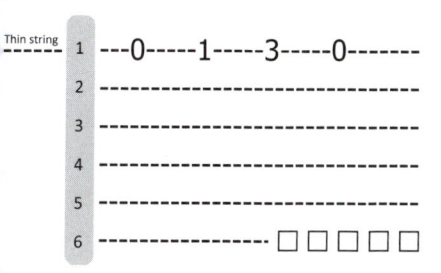

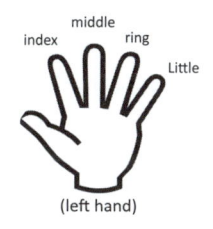

```
Thin string
------  1  ---0-----1-----3-----0-------
        2  --------------------------------
        3  --------------------------------
        4  --------------------------------
        5  --------------------------------
        6  -----------------  ☐ ☐ ☐ ☐
```

(left hand) — index, middle, ring, Little

2. "Lift off"

```
Thin string
------  1  ---0----0----1----1----2----2----3---------
        2  --------------------------------------------
        3  --------------------------------------------
        4  --------------------------------------------
        5  --------------------------------------------
        6  --------------------------------  ☐ ☐ ☐ ☐ ☐
```

3. "Ten Green Bottles" (pt 1)

Ten   green   bott - les   sit - ting   on   the   wall...

```
Thin string
------  1  ---0---0---0---4------2---0---2---4---0---
        2  --------------------------------------------
        3  --------------------------------------------
        4  --------------------------------------------
        5  --------------------------------------------
        6  --------------------------------  ☐ ☐ ☐ ☐ ☐
```

Ch2 L2 TAB

TAB lesson 2

Try and use the suggested left hand fingering (**i m r L**) to play the notes for lesson 2.

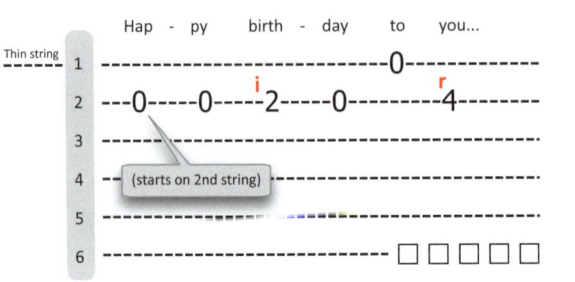

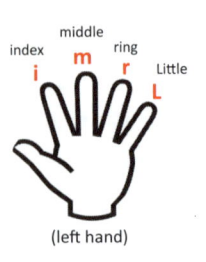

1. "Happy Birthday" (pt 1)

```
          Hap - py    birth - day    to    you...
                                     r
Thin string  1  -----------------------------0-------------
                     i                   r
             2  ---0-----0-----2-----0---------4--------
             3  --------------------------------------------
             4  --  (starts on 2nd string)  --------------
             5  --------------------------------------------
             6  --------------------------------------------
```

(left hand)
index — i
middle — m
ring — r
Little — L

2. "Jingle Bells" (pt 1)

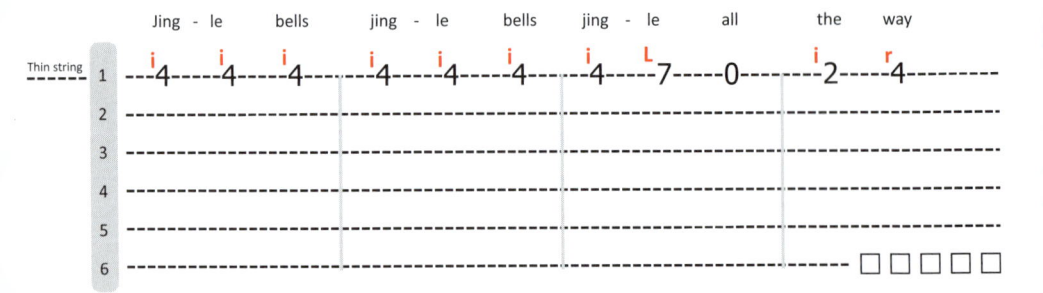

```
          Jing - le   bells   jing - le   bells   jing - le   all        the      way
             i   i    i       i    i      i       i    L               i        r
Thin string  1  -4----4----4-----4----4----4-----4----7-----0--------2-----4-------
             2  -----------------------------------------------------------------
             3  -----------------------------------------------------------------
             4  -----------------------------------------------------------------
             5  -----------------------------------------------------------------
             6  -----------------------------------------------------------------
```

3. "Old MacDonald"

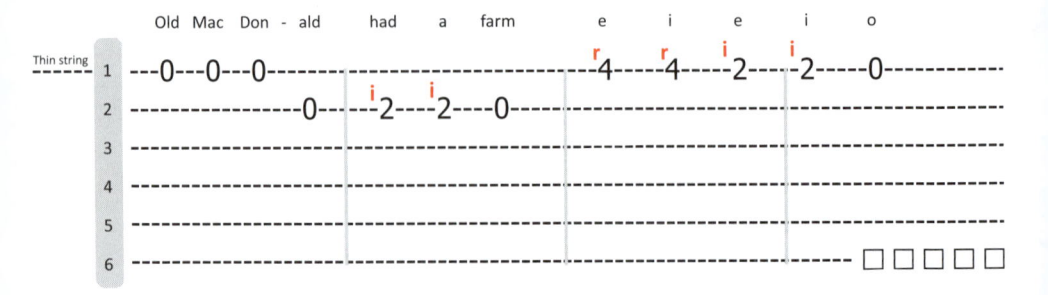

```
          Old  Mac  Don - ald   had    a    farm     e      i     e      i     o
                                                     r      r     i      i
Thin string  1  ---0---0---0----------------------------4-----4----2-----2----0-----------
                                      i     i
             2  ----------------0-----2-----2---0-----------------------------------
             3  -----------------------------------------------------------------
             4  -----------------------------------------------------------------
             5  -----------------------------------------------------------------
             6  -----------------------------------------------------------------
```

TAB lesson 3

1. "Happy Birthday" (pt 2)

```
         Hap - py   birth - day    to    you,      hap - py    birth - day    to   you...
                                    i                                          i
Thin string 1 ------------------------------0---------------------------------2---0-----
         2 ----0----0----2----0----------4----0----0----2----0------------------
         3 ------------------------------------------------------------------------
         4 ------------------------------------------------------------------------
         5 ------------------------------------------------------------------------
         6 ------------------------------------------------------------------------
```

2. "Merry Christmas" (pt 1)

```
         We  wish  you   a   mer - ry  Christ - mas we   wish   you   a   mer - ry  Christ - mas
                         i                               i     i     r     i
Thin string 1 --------0----0----2----0-----------------2----2----4----2----0-----------
         2 ---0-------------------4----2----2---------------------------4-----0----
         3 ----------------------------2----------------------------------------
         4 ------------------------------------------------------------------------
         5 ------------------------------------------------------------------------
         6 ------------------------------------------------------------------------
```

3. "Oh When the Saints" (pt 1)

```
         Oh   when   the   saints     oh   when   the   saints   oh   when   the   saints   go   mar - ching  in
              i     m    L                i     m    L                i     m    L           i          i
Thin string 1 ---0---4----5----7--------0----4----5----7--------0----4----5----7--------4----0----4----2---
         2 ------------------------------------------------------------------------
         3 ------------------------------------------------------------------------
         4 ------------------------------------------------------------------------
         5 ------------------------------------------------------------------------
         6 ------------------------------------------------------------------------
```

TAB lesson 4

1. "Ten Green Bottles" (pt 2)

```
           Ten  green  bott-les       sit - ting  on  the  wall      ten  green  bott-les       sit - ting  on  the  wall
                              r              i    i    r              i    i    i    L              m    i    m    L    i
1 ---0---0---0---4---------2---0---2---4---0-------4---4---4---7---------5---4---5---7---4----
2 ----------------------------------------------------------------------------------------------
3 ----------------------------------------------------------------------------------------------
4 ----------------------------------------------------------------------------------------------
5 ----------------------------------------------------------------------------------------------
6 ----------------------------------------------------------------------------------------------
```

2. "Jingle Bells" (full)

```
        Jingle  bells   jingle  bells   jingle  all    the  way    oh what fun    it is    to ride    in a one horse open sleigh hey!
          i    i    i    i    i    i          i    L          i    r              L    L    L          L    r    r          r    r    r    i    i    r    i    L
1 ---4--4--4------4--4--4-------4--7--0-------2--4-----------5--5--5-------5--5--4--4--------4--4--4---2--2---4--2---7---
2 ----------------------------------------------------------------------------------------------
3 ----------------------------------------------------------------------------------------------
4 ----------------------------------------------------------------------------------------------
5 ----------------------------------------------------------------------------------------------
6 ----------------------------------------------------------------------------------------------

        Jingle  bells   jingle  bells   jingle  all    the  way    oh what fun    it is    to ride    in a one horse  o - pen  sleigh!
          i    i    i    i    i    i          i    L          i    r              L    L    L          L    r    r          r    r    L    L    L    i
  ---4--4--4------4--4--4-------4--7--0-------2--4-----------5--5--5-------5--5--4--4--------4--4--7--7---5---2---0---
```

3. "Swing Low"

```
        Swing low sweet cha - ri - ot      comin' for to ca - rry me home      swing low  sweet cha - ri - ot      coming' for to      ca - rry me home
          r    r                                                 i    i    L    L          L    L    i    L                                                 r    r    i
1 ---4--0---4--0--0------------0--0--0--0--4--4--7---7----9--7--4----7--0--0-------------0--0--0--0--4--4--2--0---
2 --------------------i--2--0----------------------------------------i--2--0----------------------------
3 ----------------------------------------------------------------------------------------------
4 ----------------------------------------------------------------------------------------------
5 ----------------------------------------------------------------------------------------------
6 ----------------------------------------------------------------------------------------------
```

TAB lesson 5

1. "Happy Birthday" (full)

```
              Hap - py  birth - day  to  you,    hap - py  birth - day  to    you,    hap - py birth - day dear doo daa,  hap - py   birth - day  to   you!
                                 i                                 i                            L                         L    L    r            i
Thin string 1 ----------------0--------------------------2--0--------------------7--4--0------------5---5--4---0---2--0--
            2 --0---0--2---0----------4-----0--0--2--0-----------------0--0------------4--2------------------------------
                         r                  i                                                     r  i
            3 -----------------------------------------------------------------------------------------------------------
            4 -----------------------------------------------------------------------------------------------------------
            5 -----------------------------------------------------------------------------------------------------------
            6 -----------------------------------------------------------------------------------------------------------
```

2. "Oh When the Saints" (full)

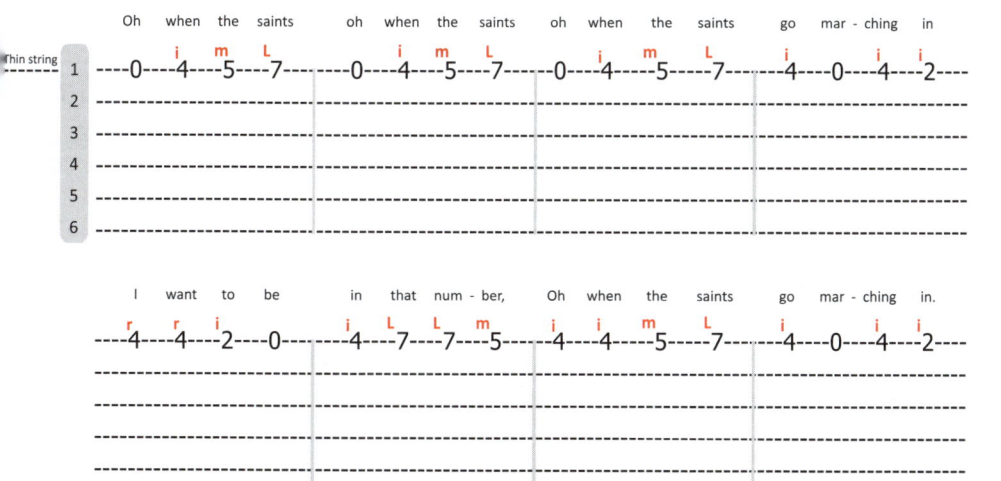

```
               Oh    when    the   saints    oh    when   the   saints    oh   when   the  saints    go   mar - ching   in
                       i    m     L                 i    m    L                 i   m    L             i           i
Thin string 1 ----0---4----5----7------0---4----5----7------0---4----5----7-----4---0---4---2----
            2 -----------------------------------------------------------------------------------------------------------
            3 -----------------------------------------------------------------------------------------------------------
            4 -----------------------------------------------------------------------------------------------------------
            5 -----------------------------------------------------------------------------------------------------------
            6 -----------------------------------------------------------------------------------------------------------

               I   want   to    be      in   that   num - ber,    Oh  when   the   saints    go   mar - ching   in.
                 r    r    i                   i   L    L    m                i   i   m    L              i            i
            1 ----4----4----2---0-------4----7----7----5-------4----4----5----7------4---0---4---2----
            2 -----------------------------------------------------------------------------------------------------------
            3 -----------------------------------------------------------------------------------------------------------
            4 -----------------------------------------------------------------------------------------------------------
            5 -----------------------------------------------------------------------------------------------------------
            6 -----------------------------------------------------------------------------------------------------------
```

3. "Merry Christmas" (pt 2)

```
              We wish you a merry Christmas  we wish you a merry   Christmas  we wish you a   merry Christmas   and a    ha - ppy   new  year
                             i                    i    r   i                     r   r   L   r    i                    i                
Thin string 1 ----0--0--2--0-------------2--2--4--2--0-----------4--4--5--4--2--0---------------2---------0---
            2 --0-------------4--2-----2---------------4------4---------------------2--0--0--2-------4---
                                   i
            3 ---------------2---------------------------0------------------------------------------------
            4 -----------------------------------------------------------------------------------------------------------
            5 -----------------------------------------------------------------------------------------------------------
            6 -----------------------------------------------------------------------------------------------------------
```

TAB lesson 6

1. "Ten Green Bottles" (full)

```
                  Ten   green  bott-les      sit-ting  on   the   wall    ten  green  bott-les     sit-ting on the wall   and  if
                                         r                                  i     i     i   L       m   i   m L   i
Thin string  1  --0----0----0----4------ --2--0---2----4--0--- --4---4---4---7--- --5-4-5--7--4---0--0---
             2  ----------------------------------------------------------------------------------------
             3  ----------------------------------------------------------------------------------------
             4  ----------------------------------------------------------------------------------------
             5  ----------------------------------------------------------------------------------------
             6  ----------------------------------------------------------------------------------------

                 one  green   bot-tle        should ac-ci-dently    fall    there'll be nine green bottles    sit-ting  on   the  wall...
                 L    L    L    i                i    r  i                                            r        i        i    r
              --9----9---7----4------  --0--2--4--2--0-------- ----------- --0--0--0--4----- --2--0---2---4--0------
                                                               i                       i
              -------------------------------------------2------ ---0--2----------------------------------
              ----------------------------------------------------------------------------------------
              ----------------------------------------------------------------------------------------
              ----------------------------------------------------------------------------------------
              ----------------------------------------------------------------------------------------
```

☐ ☐ ☐ ☐ ☐

2. Blues Scale in G (two octaves)

```
                                                         i                 i
                                                       --3----           --3----
                                            i   L                  L  i
                                          --3--6---              --6--3---
                                     i  r  L                              L  r  i
                                   --3--5--6---                         --6--5--3---
                               i   r                                              r  i
Thin string  1  -----------  --3--5---                                          --5--3----
                         i   m  r                                                    r  m  i
             2  -------- --3--4--5---                                              --5--4--3----
                  i   L                                                                        L  i
             3  --3--6-----                                                                --6--3---
             4  ----------
             5  ----------
             6  ----------
```

☐ ☐ ☐ ☐ ☐

3. "The Grand Old Duke of York"

```
                  Oh the grand old Duke of York     he had  10,000    men     he marched them up to the top of the hill and he marched them down again
                 L  m   i                           i    i    i    i           i   r  r  r  r  L  L  L     L  L    r                    r
Thin string 1 --7--5--4--0-0-0-0------- --0--2--2--2--2--2--- --2-4-4-4-4-5-5-5-5--- --5-5--4--0--2-----0----
                                                                                                                               r
            2 -----------------------------------------------------------------------------------4--------
            3 -----------------------------------------------------------------------------------------
            4 -----------------------------------------------------------------------------------------
            5 -----------------------------------------------------------------------------------------
            6 -----------------------------------------------------------------------------------------
```

☐ ☐ ☐ ☐ ☐

TAB lesson 7

1. "Blues Solo" (pt 1)

b = bend the string

```
Thin string
 1  ---12----10---------------------------------------------------------
 2  ----------------12---11---10-----------------------------8-----b8----
 3  --------------------------------b12----9---------7----9-----------9--
 4  ---------------------------------------------------------------------
 5  ---------------------------------------------------------------------
 6  ---------------------------------------------------------------------
```

2. "Blues Solo Bass" (pt 1)

```
Thin string
 1  ---------------------------------------------------------------------
 2  ---------------------------------------------------------------------
 3  ---------------------------------------------------------------------
 4  -------------------------5----------8----7----5---------------5------
 5  --------------------5-----7--------7----------------7----5----7----7-
 6  ---0---3---5---5-s-7-------------------------------------------------
```

s = slide between 5th and 7th fret

3. "Give Me Oil in My Lamp" (pt 1)

Give me oil in my lamp keep me burning give me oil in my lamp   I pray   give me oil in my lamp keep me burning keep me burning till the break of day

```
Thin string
 1  -----------------------------------------------------------------------------------
 2  --0--0--0-------------------0--0--0------------------0--0--0---------------0--0----
 3  ---------1------------------------1---------1-----------------1---------1------2--1
 4  ------------4--2--4--2--2------------4--2----4--------------4--2--2--2--4---------4--2-
 5  ---------------------4---------------------------4-----------------------------------
 6  -----------------------------------------------------------------------------------
```

TAB lesson 8

1. "Blues Solo" (full)

```
Thin string
         1  --12--10----------------------------------------------------------------
         2  ---------12--11--10-----------m-------m-------------------------------
         3  ------------------b12--9----7--9-------9------9--7--------------------
         4  ----------------------------------------------------9--8--7--5--------
         5  -----------------------------------------------------------------7--5-
         6  ------------------------------------------------------------7--6--5--b3--0--
```

b = bend the note

2. "Blues Solo Bass" (full)

```
Thin string
         1  -------------------------------------------------------------------10--12--
         2  -------------------------------------------------8---8--10--11--12--------
         3  -----------------------------------------7--9------9----------------------
         4  -----------------5---8--7--5------5--7--8--9------------------------------
         5  -----------5--7--7-----------7--5--7-----7--------------------------------
         6  --0--3--5--5s7------------------------------------------------------------
```

s = slide between 5th and 7th fret

3. "Auld Lang Syne"

Should auld acquaintance be forgot   and   never brought to mind should auld acquaintance be forgot and   auld   lang   syne
```
Thin string
         1  ----0--0--0--4--2--0--2-----4--2--0--0--4--7--9-----9--7--4--4--0--2--0--2-----4--2--0-----------0----
         2  ---0-----------------------------------------------------------------------------------2--2--0------
         3  ------------------------------------------------------------------------------------------------
         4  ------------------------------------------------------------------------------------------------
         5  ------------------------------------------------------------------------------------------------
         6  ------------------------------------------------------------------------------------------------
```

For auld   lang syne, my dear, for   auld   lang   syne,   we'll take a cup of kindness yet, for   auld   lang   syne.
```
---9--7--4--4--0--2--0--2-----9--7--4--4--0--2-----9--7--4--4--0--2--0--2-----4--2--0-----------0----
-----------------------------------------------------------------------------------2--2--0------
```

TAB lesson 9

1. "Merry Christmas" (full)

TAB lesson 10

1. The G major scale (two octaves and back)

```
Thin string
  1  -----------------------------------------i-2---m-3-----i-2-------------------------------
  2  -----------------------------m---L---3---5-------------L-5--m-3-----------------------
  3  ---------------------i---r---L-2---4---5-----------------------5---4---2---------------
  4  -------------i-2---r-L-4---5-----------------------------------------5---4---2---------
  5  ----i-m-L-2---3---5-----------------------------------------------------L-5---3---i-2--m----
  6  m-L-3---5-----------------------------------------------------------------------5---3--
```
☐ ☐ ☐ ☐ ☐

2. "Yankee Doodle" (full)

```
Thin string
  1  ---0-0-i-2-r-4-i-0-r-4-2-----------0-0-i-2-r-4-0-----------0-0-i-2-r-4-L-5-r-4-2-0-----------0-------------0-----
  2  ---------------------0---------------------r-4---0----------------------------------r-4-0-i-2-r-4---
  3
  4
  5
  6
```

```
                                        0                            0          0---i-2---0-----0---
  i-r-i-r-i-r
  -2---4---2---i-4-----0-i-2-0-------------0-----i-r-i-r-i-----2---4-2-0-2---4-----r-4-------
                              -2---1-------
```
☐ ☐ ☐ ☐ ☐

3. "God Rest Ye Merry Gentlemen"

```
Thin string
  1  -----i-2--i-2--0------------0--i-2----------i-2--i-2--0------------0--i-2-----
  2  --0-0-----------m-3-2-0-----0--2-3--------0-0-----------m-3-2-0-----0-i-m-2-3-
  3  ---------------------2---------------------------------------2----------------
  4
  5
  6
```

```
  i-m     i-m-m-L-i                       i-m  i-i                  i-m-m-L-i
  -2-3-0--2-3-5-7-2-0-----------0-----2-3-2-2-0-----------0--0-2-3-5-7-2-0-m-i-
                  m   i-m  m                m   m-i                           3-2-0-
                  -3-0-2-3-3-------3-2-0-3-2-0-3
```
☐ ☐ ☐ ☐ ☐

TAB treat

1. "E Squeeze" riff (bronze)

```
         m                    m   m                m
thin string
1      --8b-------------------8---8b---------------8b----------------------------
2      ------r-----i---r---i-----------r---i---r-----------r---i---r---i---m---i-
3      ------9-----7---9---7---9-------9---7---9-----------9---7---9---7-----8---7---5---
4                                                                              r
5                                                                              7
6
```
b = bend the note (up)

pause!

2. "E Squeeze" riff (silver)

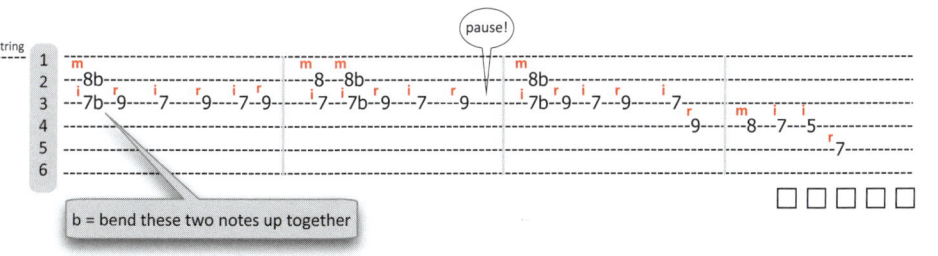

```
         m                    m   m                m
thin string
1      --8b-------------------8---8b---------------8b----------------------------
2      --7b--9---i-r-i-r-i-r--i--7b--9--i-r--i--r--7b--9--i-r-i-r-i
3      ------9---7---9---7---9-----7--9----7---9-----9---7---9---7---r--m--i
4                                                                   9---8---7---5
5                                                                              r
6                                                                              7
```
b = bend these two notes up together

pause!

3. "E Squeeze" riff (gold)

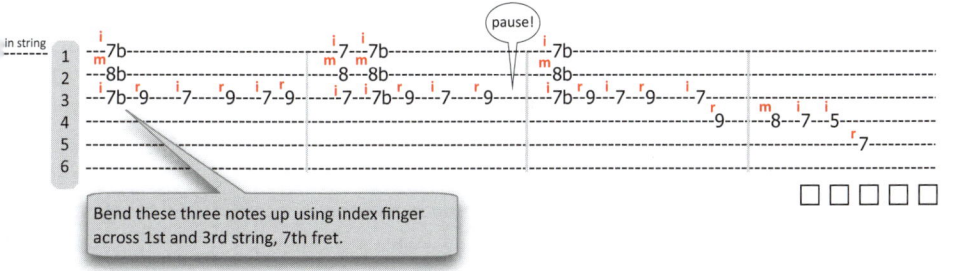

```
        i                  i    i                 i
        m                  m    m                 m
1     --7b-----------------7---7b----------------7b---------------------
2     --8b-----------------8---8b----------------8b---------------------
3     --7b--9--i-r-i-r-i-r-i--7b--9-i-r-i-r-i-r--7b--9--i-r-i-r-i
4                                                    r--m--i
4                                                    9---8---7---5
5                                                                 r
6                                                                 7
```
Bend these three notes up using index finger across 1st and 3rd string, 7th fret.

pause!

TAB debrief

Great achievement for getting this far! You have now learnt the basics of TAB, and hopefully have increased your confidence to tackle more challenging songs.

It is really all about practice and repetition from now on.
The more TABs you attempt, the quicker your fingers will adapt, and the easier it will become. You may notice more difficult looking TAB songs online and be tempted to panic, but if you take things very slowly one bar at a time, you will begin to work them out slowly but surely.

Numbers on top of each other (or in line with each other) simply mean you have to play them at the same time (down strumming as a full chord or in the case of two or three notes, finger picking them together). Below is an example of the chord of E.

The E chord in TAB

```
1  -----0-----
2  -----0-----
3  -----2-----
4  -----3-----
5  -----3-----
6  -----0-----
```

You will also notice other TAB symbols on the more difficult songs (vibrato, hammer-ons, pull offs, and slides) – they all refer to particular techniques to create different sounds from the guitar. Check out other people's various tutorials on YouTube to master these as you progress in your own playing.

In the meantime, keep playing little and often, and your fingers will learn to get where they are supposed to be, quickly and cleanly. Experiment with rhythm by playing the notes as if you were humming or singing it, with some notes lasting longer or shorter than others.

Above all, enjoy! Remember this is not a competition or race, but a step by step, little by little process of learning to play one of the world's most versatile instruments.

3 How to Play Chords

Learning to play chords and moving quickly between them is a top priority for a beginner.

Many guitarists lose heart because they never seem to master the quick chord change.

The key is repetition. Move enough times between E and A and your fingers will soon remember. In a very short while you will not even have to look at your fingers; they will know what to do!

Starting with small steps is often the best way as struggling through a whole song before you are ready can be frustrating. As you work through the ten chord lessons, your confidence and ability will increase as you progress.

Page

Chords lesson 1: The chord of Easy E 35

Chords lesson 2: Easy E and A 36

Chords lesson 3: Easy E, A, and B7 37

Chords lesson 4: E chord 38

Chords lesson 5: E and A 39

Chords lesson 6: E, A, and B7 40

Chords lesson 7: E, A, B7, and D 41

Chords lesson 8: The 16 chord block – E, A, B7, D, G, and C 42

Chords lesson 9: The 16 chord block without chord boxes 44

Chords lesson 10: The 16 chord block strumming styles 45

intro Chords

Chords intro: How to read a chord box

The chord box in this book is set out from the player's point of view, so if you lay your guitar flat on your lap, it will be very similar.

Remember, with the guitar in the playing position on your thigh, the thick string (6th) is closest to your face.

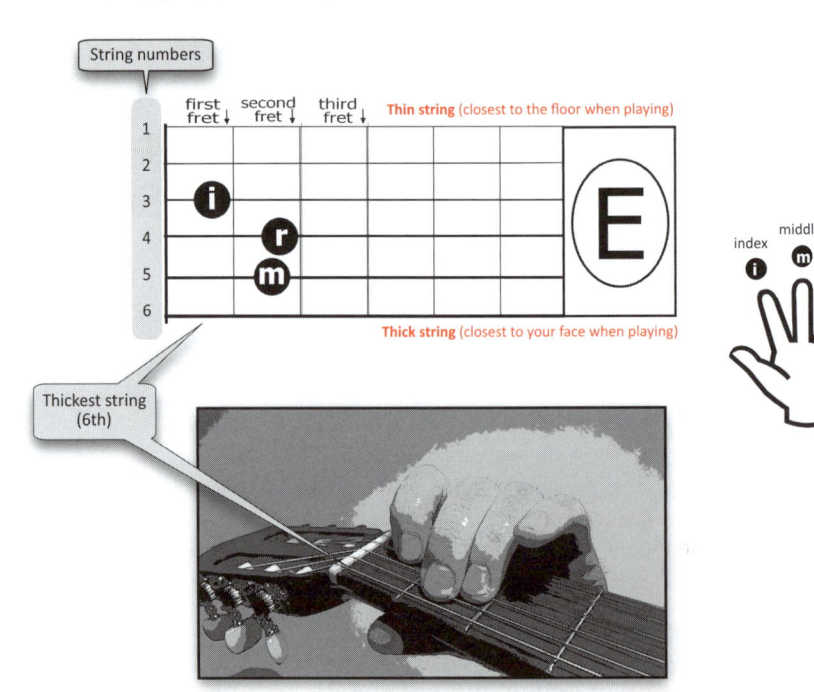

String numbers

first fret ↓ second fret ↓ third fret ↓

Thin string (closest to the floor when playing)

E

index **i**   middle **m**   ring **r**   Little **L**

Thick string (closest to your face when playing)

Thickest string (6th)

At each level there are three self-evaluation check squares that help you chart your own progress.

☑ (attempted this level a few times)
☑ ☑ (definitely seeing progress at this level)
☑ ☑ ☑ (can change between chords quickly and in time)   L1 check: ☐ ☐ ☐

Top Tip
Remember, as you progress through the lessons it's all about **quality** not speed.
1. Press down fingertips, just behind the frets.
2. Keep your down strum slow and even – it's much better to be **slow and smooth** than quick and untidy.

Chords Ch3 L1

Chords lesson 1: The chord of Easy E

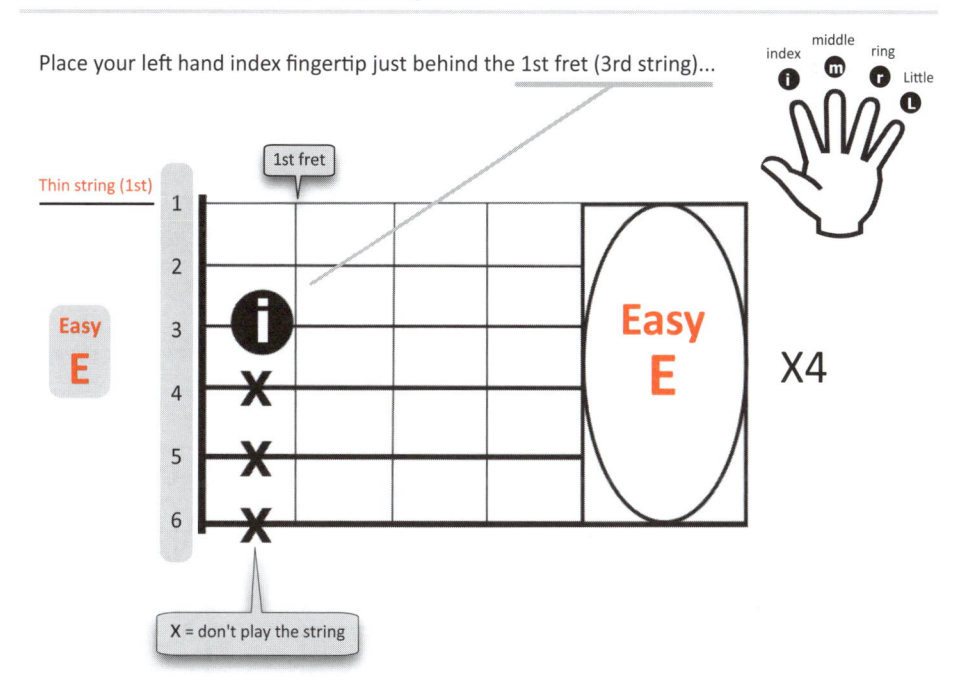

Place your left hand index fingertip just behind the 1st fret (3rd string)...

index — middle — ring — Little

Thin string (1st)

1st fret

Easy E

Easy E

X4

X = don't play the string

...and with your right hand thumb, down strum the 3rd, 2nd, and 1st string — **four times.**

L1 check: ☐ ☐ ☐

Ch3 L2 Chords

Chords lesson 2: The chords of Easy E and A

With your right-hand thumb, down strum the 1st, 2nd, and 3rd strings – **four times each.**

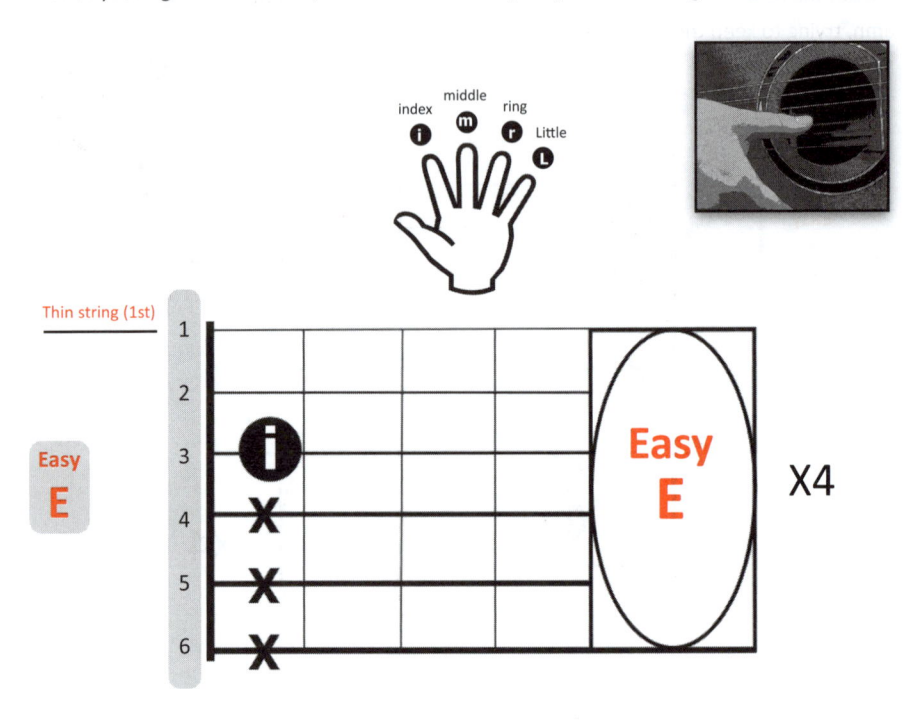

index — middle — ring — Little

Thin string (1st)

Easy E

1					
2					
3	**i**				Easy E
4	x				
5	x				
6	x				

X4

Easy A

1					
2		**m**			
3		**i**			Easy A
4	x				
5	x				
6	x				

X4

L2 check: ☐ ☐ ☐

Chords Ch3 L3

Chords lesson 3: The chords of Easy E, A, and B7

Check out the new chord of B7 – then down strum (four times each) the whole column, trying to keep the rhythm steady and smooth throughout.

Thin string (1st)

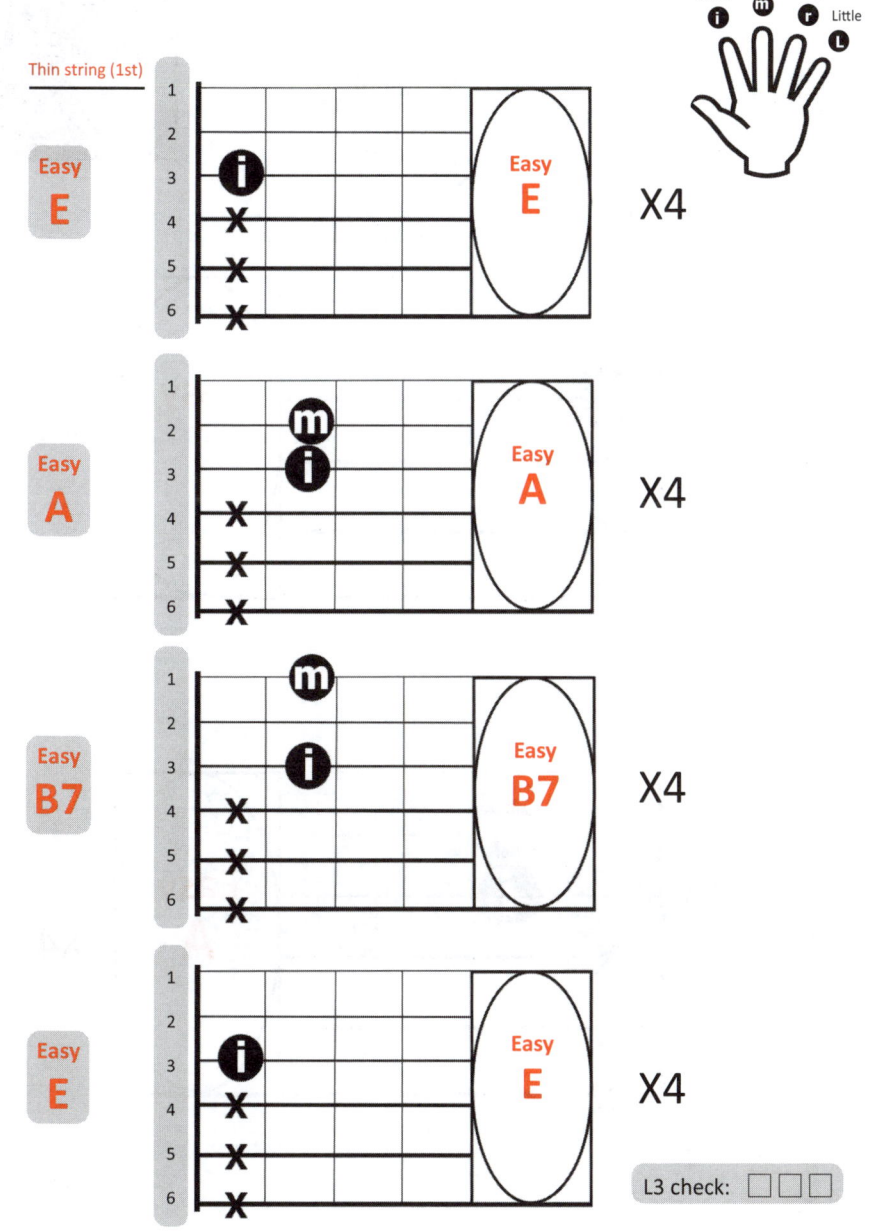

Easy E — X4

Easy A — X4

Easy B7 — X4

Easy E — X4

L3 check: ☐ ☐ ☐

Ch3 L4 Chords

Chords lesson 4: The chord of E

Now let's use all six strings with the full chord of E.

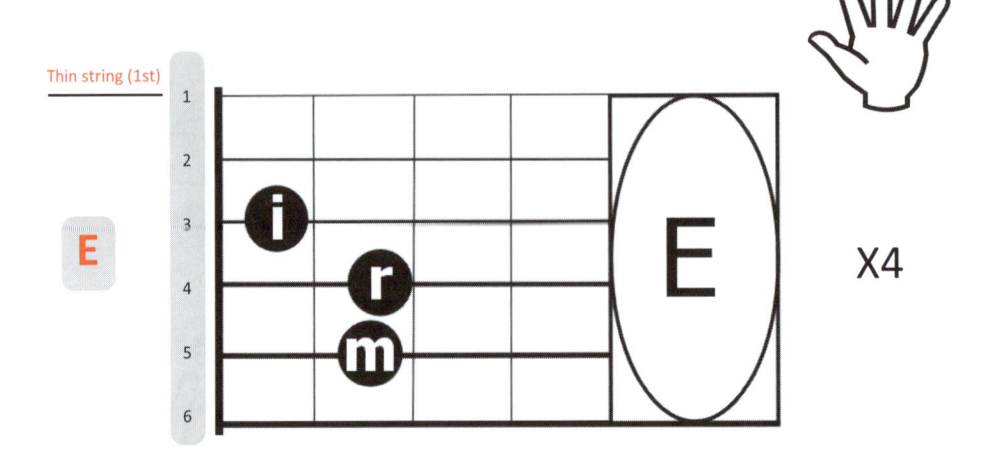

index — **i**
middle — **m**
ring — **r**
Little — **L**

Thin string (1st)

E — X4

...and this is your view of your fingers.

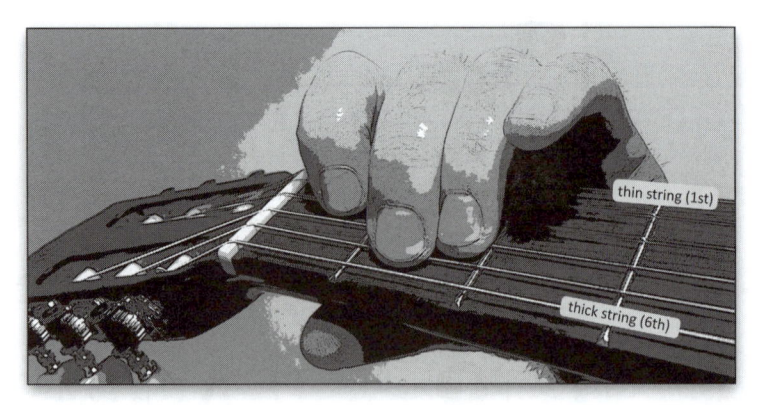

thin string (1st)

thick string (6th)

L4 check: ☐ ☐ ☐

Top Tip: To become confident with this chord, try using the **Hand Behind Technique:** Start with the left hand behind your back – count '3,2,1, go' and then see how long it takes you to play the chord cleanly. Keep repeating this until you reach the target time of under five seconds.

Chords **Ch3 L5**

Chords lesson 5: The chords of E and A

Learning to change quickly between these two chords will help you change between any two chords;

While keeping a steady beat, the goal is to change chords smoothly without pausing (i.e. keeping your right arm swinging without having to pause to wait for the left hand fingers to get to the next chord shape).

The key is repetition: Put the timer on for two minutes at a time, and just keep changing over and over and over – E, A, E, A, and so on. However boring this exercise is, you are training your fingers to change shapes. Three repetitions of two minutes a day for a week, and you will have mastered this chord change for life.

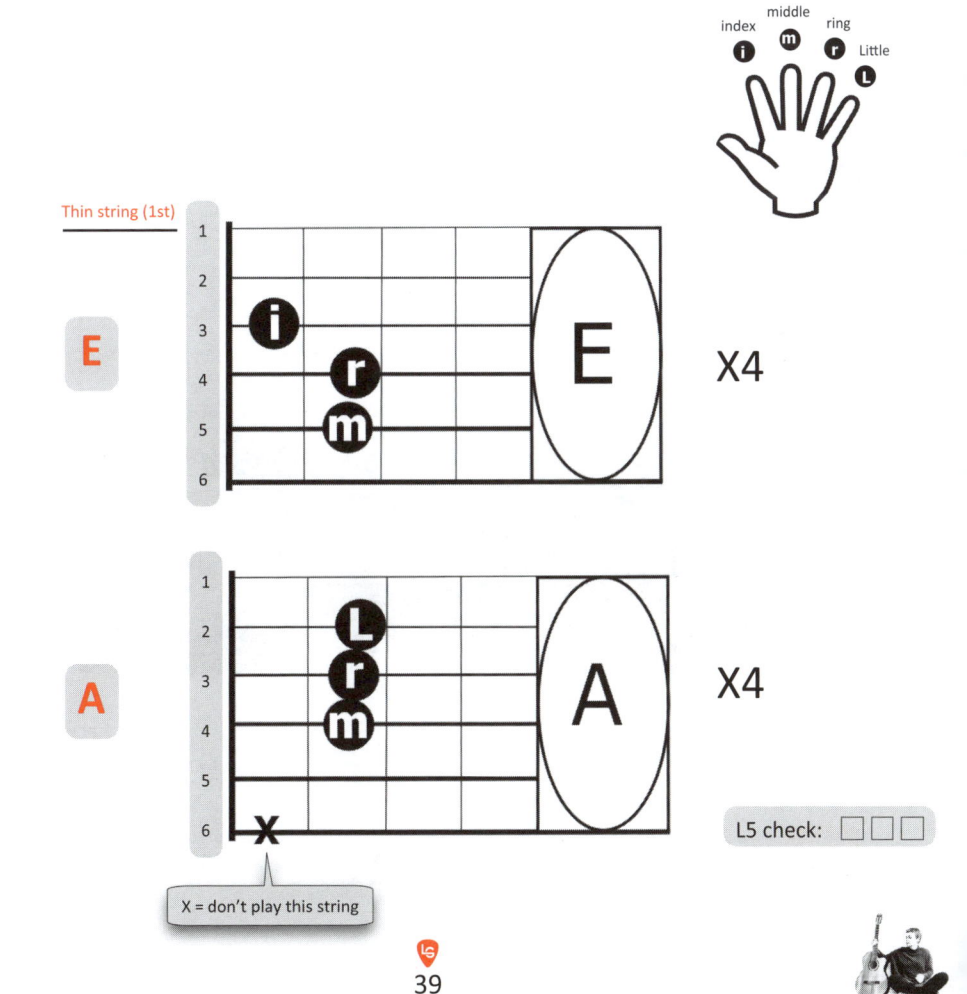

index — **i**
middle — **m**
ring — **r**
Little — **L**

Thin string (1st)

E × 4

A × 4

X = don't play this string

L5 check: ☐ ☐ ☐

39

Chords lesson 6: The chords of E, A, and B7

E, A, B7, and back to E – try to down strum these four chords, four times each, slowly and smoothly in under a minute.

E — E x4

A — A x4

B7 — B7 x4

E — E x4

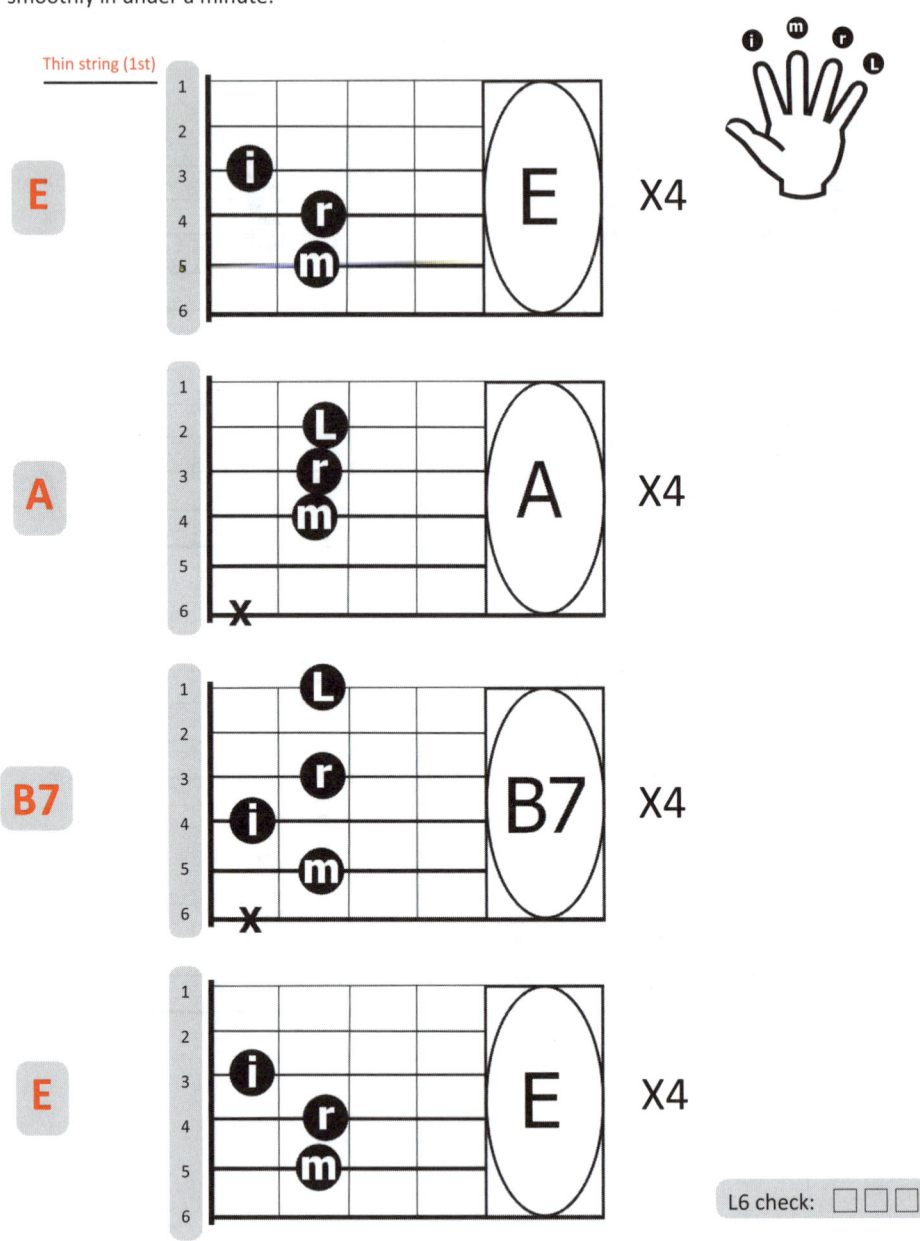

L6 check: ☐ ☐ ☐

Chords Ch3 L7

Chords lesson 7: The chords of E, A, B7, and D

Introducing the new chord of D – try to down strum these eight chords, four times each, slowly and smoothly in under a minute.

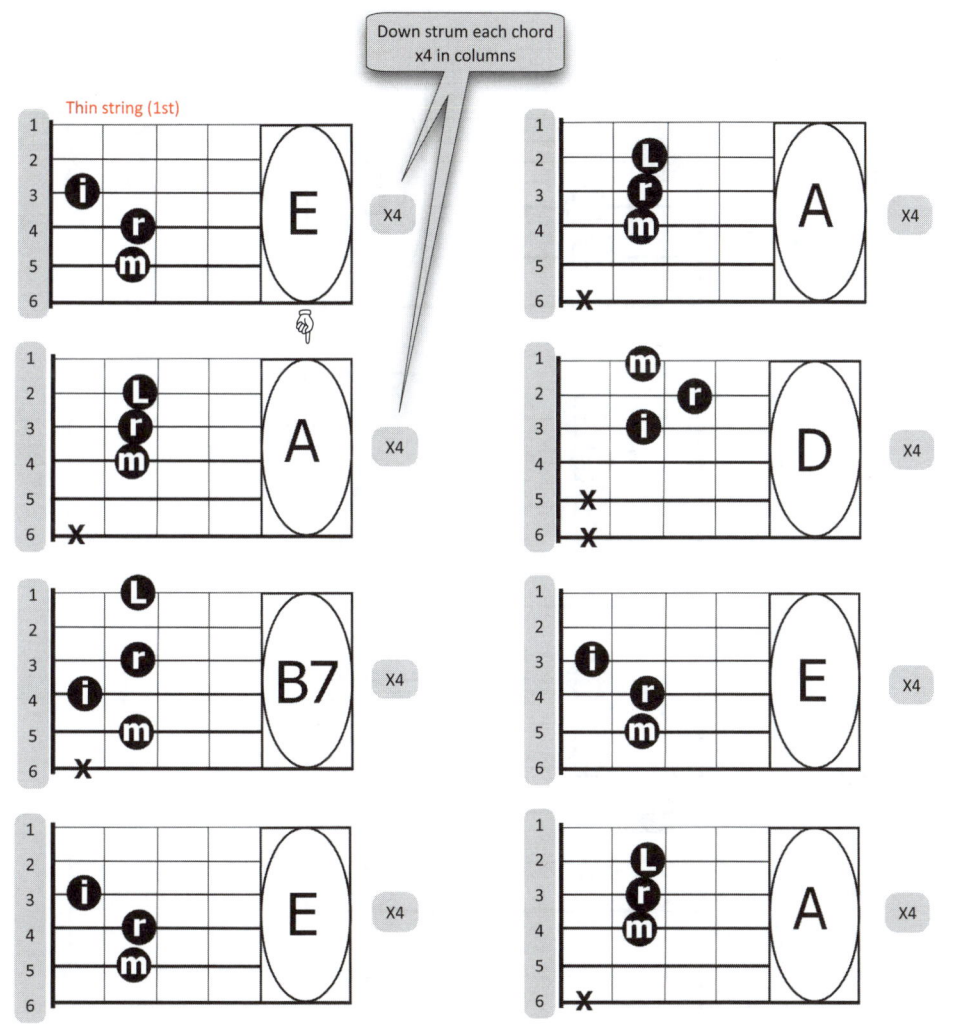

Down strum each chord x4 in columns

Thin string (1st)

E (i on 3rd fret string 5, r on 4th fret string 4, m on 4th fret string 3) X4

A (L, r, m on 2nd fret strings 4, 3, 2) X4

A (L, r, m on 2nd fret) X4

D (m on 2nd fret string 3, i on 2nd fret string 1, r on 3rd fret string 2) X4

B7 (L on 2nd fret, r on 2nd fret, i on 1st fret, m on 2nd fret) X4

E (i, r, m) X4

E (i, r, m) X4

A (L, r, m) X4

L7 target time: under 1 minute

DATE:				
TIME:				

L7 check: ☐ ☐ ☐

Watch the videos
www.loveguitar.co.uk

Chords lesson 8: The 16 chord block: E, A, B7, D, G, and C

These are the six basic chords learnt so far incorporated into a 16 chord structure. The 16 Chord Block is a really useful training exercise using the most common chords within the key families of E, A, D, and G.

Down strum each chord (X4) down the page **in columns**.

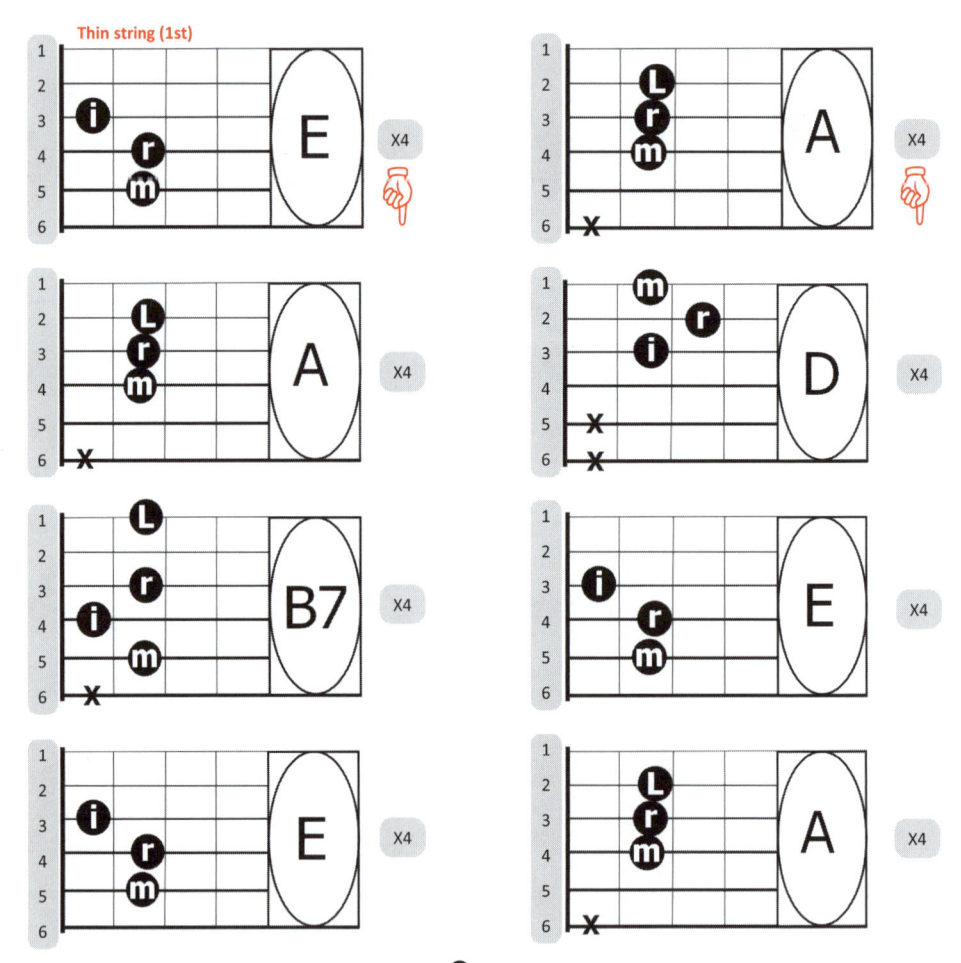

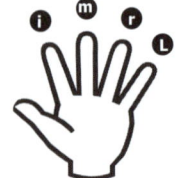

Chords **Ch3 L8**

> **Top Tip**
> Level 8 goal: down strum each chord (x4) in under a minute, as smoothly as possible.
> Don't worry if you are well outside this time to begin with. Persevere and you will become quicker and more confident, and eventually you'll be able to down strum one chord every second – this is the tempo of 60 beats per minute (BPM). Use a metronome to help you keep in time.

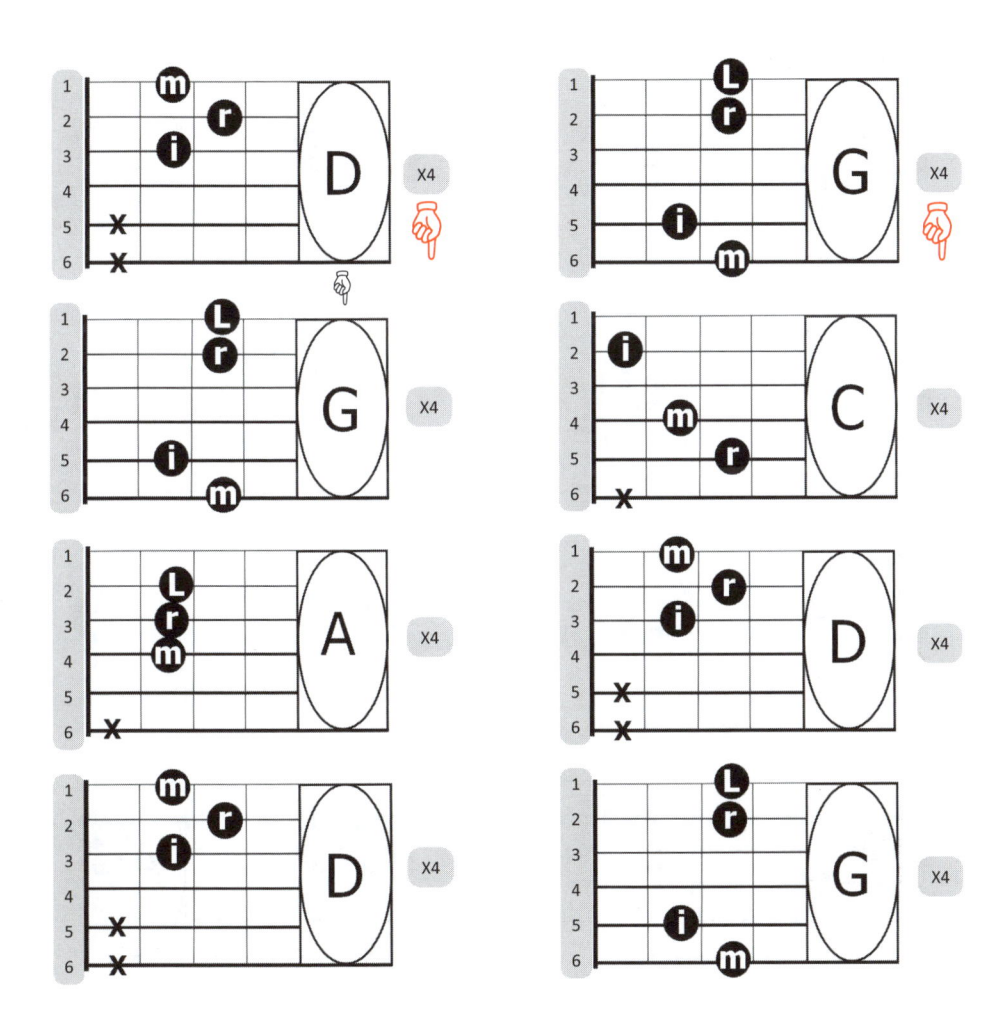

D X4

G X4

G X4

C X4

A X4

D X4

D X4

G X4

L8 target time: under 1 minute

DATE:					
TIME:					

L8 check: ☐ ☐ ☐

43

Ch3 L9 Chords

Chords lesson 9: The 16 chord block without chord boxes

At this point you'll need to start learning the chord shapes off by heart.

This time, down strum the chords (x4) across the page **in rows**.

X4	X4	X4	X4
E ☞	**A**	**B7**	**E**
X4	X4	X4	X4
A	**D**	**E**	**A**
X4	X4	X4	X4
D	**G**	**A**	**D**
X4	X4	X4	X4
G	**C**	**D**	**G**

L9 target time: under 1 minute

DATE:						
TIME:						

L9 check: ☐ ☐ ☐

Chords Ch3 L10

Chords lesson 10: The 16 chord block strumming patterns

Once you're confident with changing between chords using down strums, we can now try different strumming patterns which add variety and dynamics to your playing.

Lesson 10 goal: to strum the 16 chord block using each strumming pattern (shown below) in under a minute (i.e. four minutes for all four patterns), as smoothly as possible.

E	A	B7	E
A	D	E	A
D	G	A	D
G	C	D	G

Strumming patterns (1234's = down strums, 'ands' = upstrums – see p14)

1. 1 and 2 and 3 and 4 and
2. 1   2 and 3 and 4 and
3. 1   2   3 and 4 and
4. 1 and 2 and   and   and

L10 target time: under 4 minutes

DATE:					
TIME:					

L10 check: ☐ ☐ ☐

Chords debrief

Good work reaching this point!

The end goal of this chapter is smooth strumming with clean and tidy chord changes. If you can achieve this with these six chords within the 16 chord block, you can achieve it with any chord sequence.

However choppy and awkward your strumming feels at the moment, I guarantee that if you play through all four patterns on level 10 twice a day (around ten minutes) you'll see a dramatic difference in your playing within just three weeks.

Remember you are only breaking in your fingers once. There will come a time when you will have mastered it – and if you take a break, muscles have memories; a few days brushing up and your fingers will soon remember where they need to go.

There are many guitarists who dabble with chords, but few who are confident and strum smoothly and effortlessly without the need to look at their fingers. These are the people who have put in the time to learn well. Be that person – **learn to play simple things well** before moving on – you'll never regret the time you spent getting the basics right. You will start as a slave, but gradually you will become the master!

4 How to Finger Pick

Whichever way you look at it, finger picking is fiddly – but it is one of the most rewarding skills you can learn on the guitar. Throughout this chapter we will focus on the right hand fingers. The left hand will simply be playing the same chords we learned in Chapter 3.

Remember for the right hand:

The thumb always looks after the 6th, 5th, or 4th string.
The index finger always looks after the 3rd string.
The middle finger always looks after the 2nd string.
The ring finger always looks after the 1st string.*

                                                                                                        Page

Intro: Basic finger picking using the 1st, 2nd, and 3rd string 48

FP lesson 1: Finger picking Easy E 49

FP lesson 2: FP Easy E and A 50

FP lesson 3: FP Easy E, A, and B7 51

FP lesson 4: FP E chord 52

FP lesson 5: FP E and A 53

FP lesson 6: FP E, A, and B7 54

FP lesson 7: FP E, A, B7, and D 55

FP lesson 8: FP The 16 chord block – E, A, B7, D, G, and C 56

FP lesson 9: FP The 16 chord block without chord diagrams 58

FP lesson 10: The 16 CB alternative finger picking styles 59

* No work for the RH FP little finger in this book, apart from providing a useful support for the hand on the sound board.

Watch the videos
www.loveguitar.co.uk

intro Finger picking

Finger picking intro: Basic finger picking using the 1st, 2nd, and 3rd string

First of all, let's look at the basic finger picking pattern you'll be using for lessons 1-3. This is sometimes referred to as the 'free stroke'.

1. Rest your right hand thumb on the thickest string (6th)

2. Place your index finger underneath the 3rd string and pluck it (the finger moves in a sweeping motion towards the wrist).

Now do the same with your middle finger on the 2nd string.

Now pluck the 1st string using your ring finger...

...and then lastly plucking the 2nd string again with your middle finger.

Ring **R** Middle **M** Index **I** Thumb **T**

Right hand (finger picking)

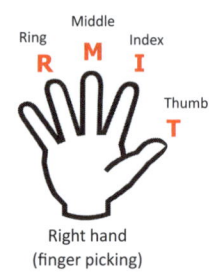

Finger pick in this order: **I, M, R, M** (X2)

This is what you have just played – with your RH thumb resting on the thick string. Just practise playing this sequence through over and over until it's beginning to sound smooth and flowing.

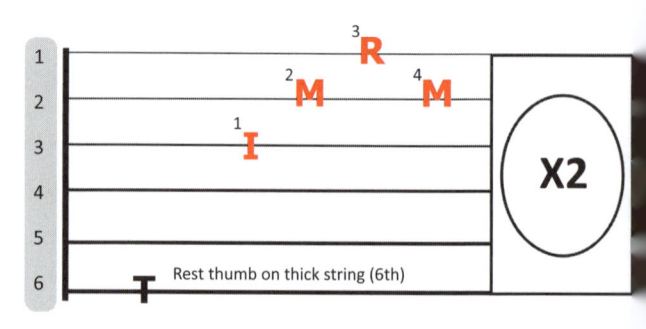

Rest thumb on thick string (6th)

X2

48

Finger picking lesson 1: Finger picking Easy E

Play Easy E with your left hand index finger.

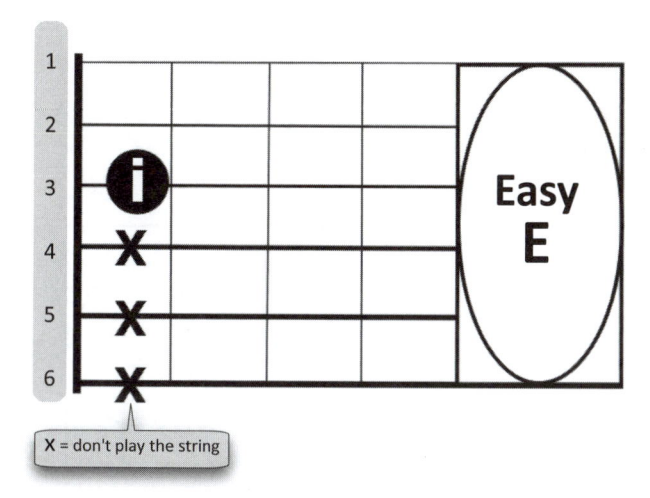

X = don't play the string

While resting your right hand thumb on the 6th string for stability, finger pick this pattern with your index/middle and ring finger in this order: **I, M, R, M** (X2)

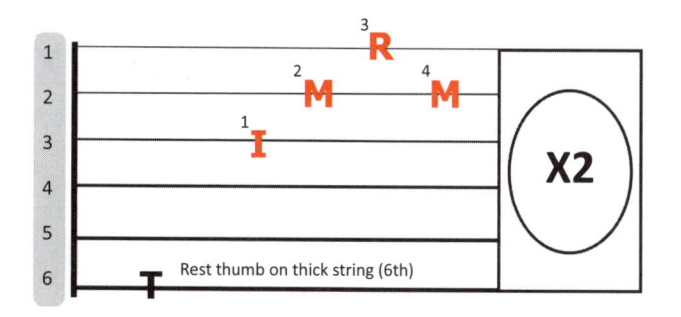

Rest thumb on thick string (6th)

Self evaluation check squares

At the end of every lesson there are three self-evaluation check squares that help you chart your own progress.

☑ (attempted this lesson a few times)
☑ ☑ (definitely seeing progress at this level)
☑ ☑ ☑ (can FP the patterns between chords smoothly and in time)   L1 check: ☐ ☐ ☐

Finger picking lesson 2: Easy E and Easy A

Finger pick both these chords as smoothly and evenly as possible.

Finger pick order: **I, M, R, M** (X2)

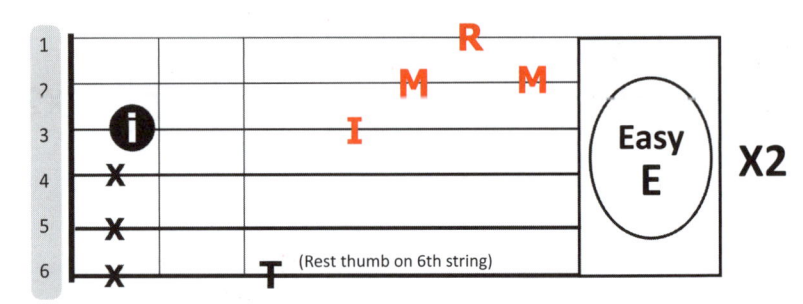

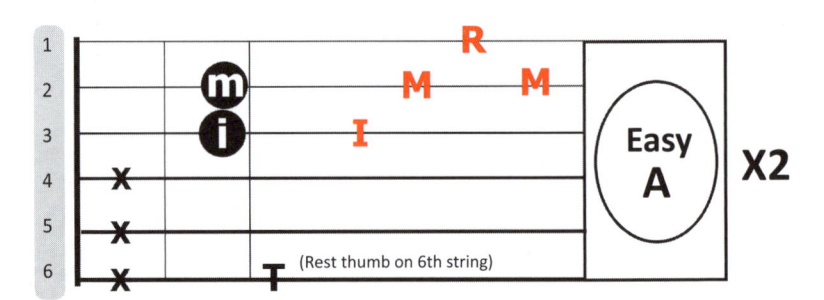

Easy E — (Rest thumb on 6th string) — Easy E X2

Easy A — (Rest thumb on 6th string) — Easy A X2

L2 check: ☐ ☐ ☐

Finger picking lesson 3: Easy E, A, and B7

This lesson adds the new chord of Easy B7.

Finger pick the pattern slowly and in time.

Easy E, A, B7, and then back to Easy E. Finger pick in this order: **I, M, R, M** (X2)

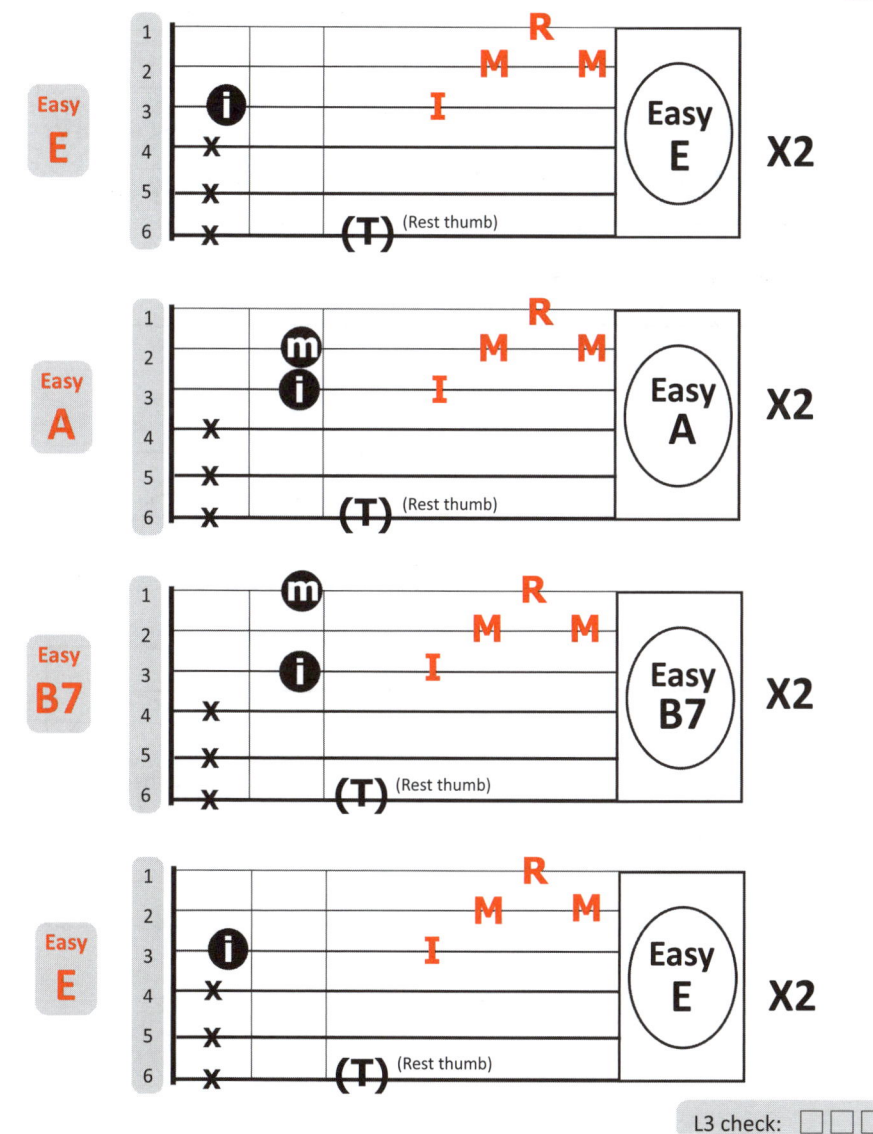

Easy E — (Rest thumb) — X2

Easy A — (Rest thumb) — X2

Easy B7 — (Rest thumb) — X2

Easy E — (Rest thumb) — X2

L3 check: ☐ ☐ ☐

Finger picking lesson 4: The chord of E

For this lesson we're looking at the full chord of E.

This time we start off with the RH thumb plucking the 6th (thickest) string first.

Try and keep your hand still and floating while the fingers do the work.

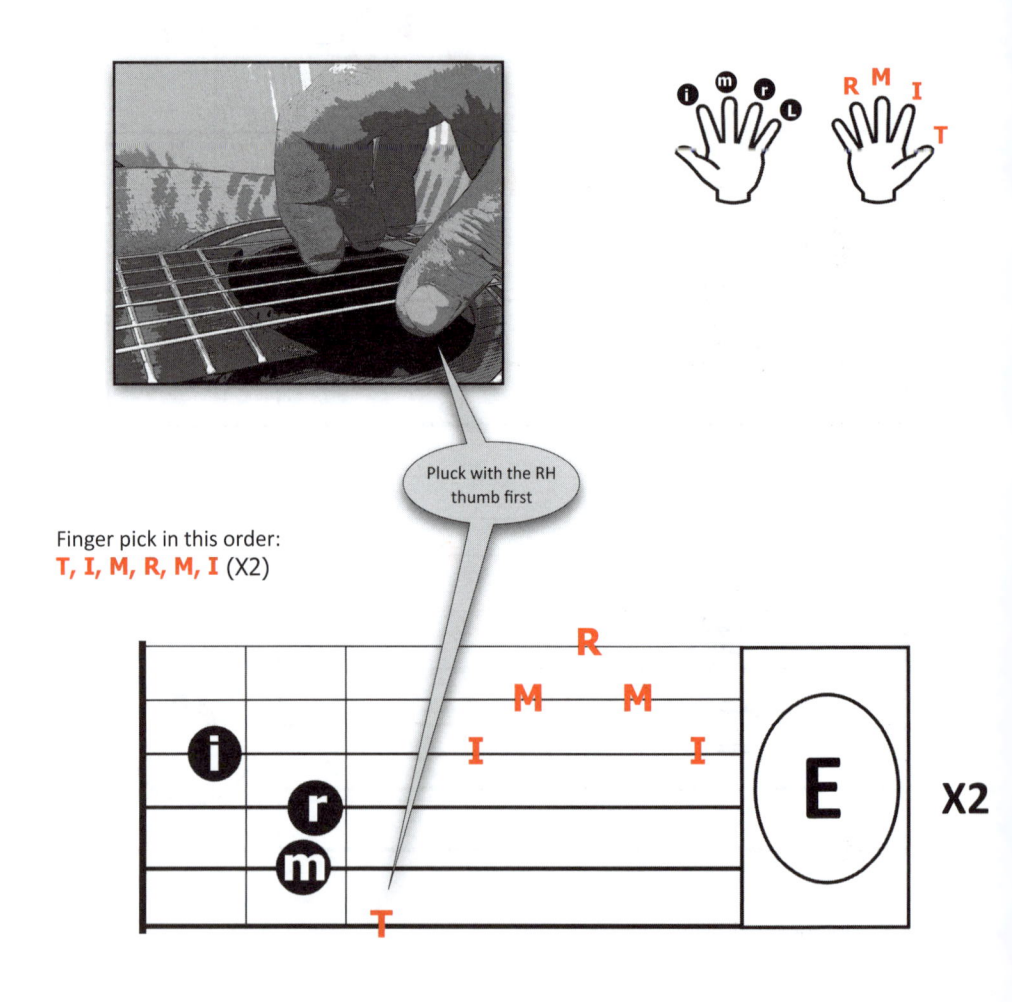

Pluck with the RH thumb first

Finger pick in this order:
T, I, M, R, M, I (X2)

E X2

L4 check:

Finger picking lesson 5: The chords of E and A

Now finger pick the chords of E then A – playing the pattern twice through each chord.

Try and pluck the notes cleanly, slowly, and evenly.

The target time is 15 - 20 seconds.

E ×2

A ×2

Thumb plucks 5th string!

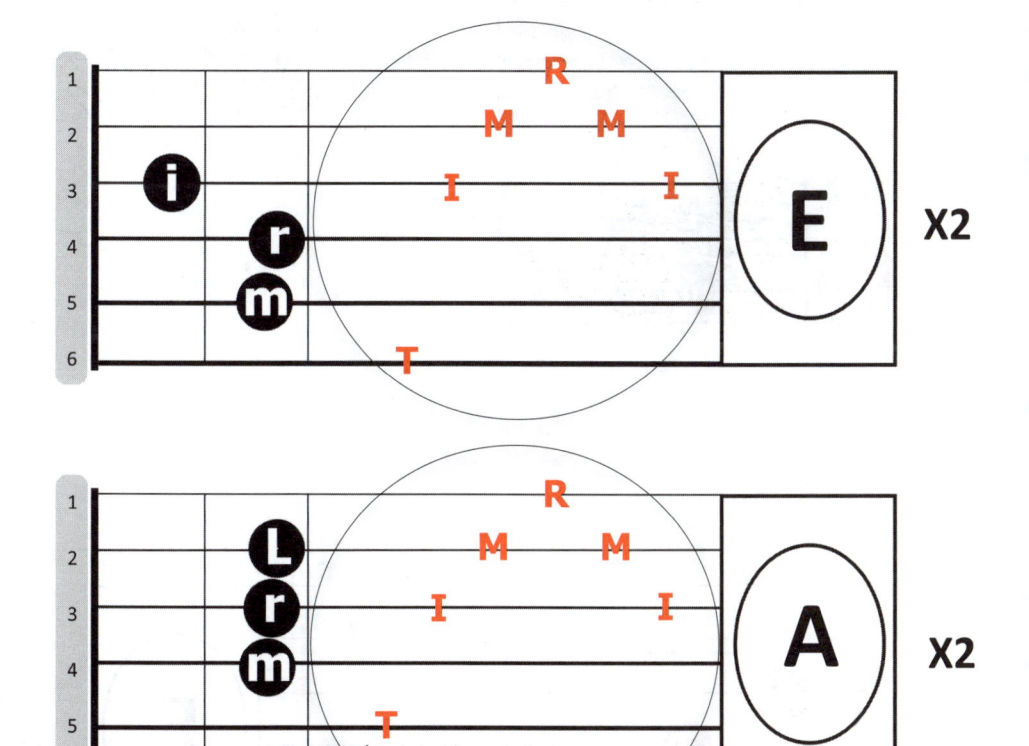

L5 check: ☐ ☐ ☐

Watch the videos
www.loveguitar.co.uk

Ch4 L6 Finger picking

Finger picking lesson 6: The chords of E, A, and B7

Repeat this page until the notes sound even and smooth flowing.

FP order: **T, I, M, R, M, I**

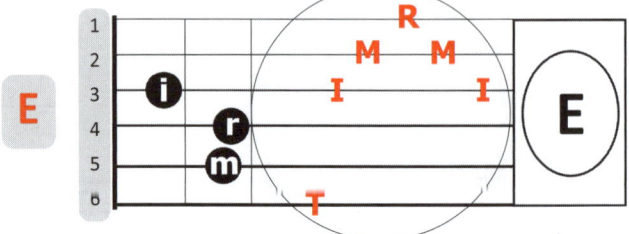

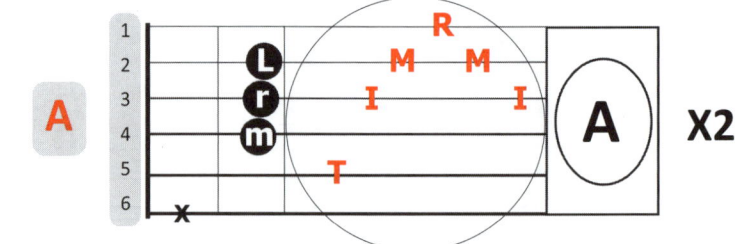

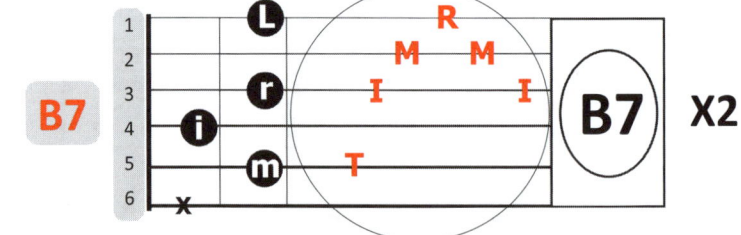

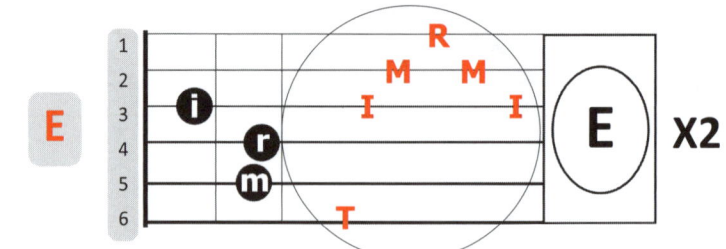

E — E X2

A — A X2

B7 — B7 X2

E — E X2

L6 target time: under 1 minute

DATE:					
TIME:					

L6 check: ☐ ☐ ☐

54

Finger picking level 7: The chords of E, A, B7, and D

Finger picking each chord pattern twice, repeat this page until the notes sound even and smooth flowing.

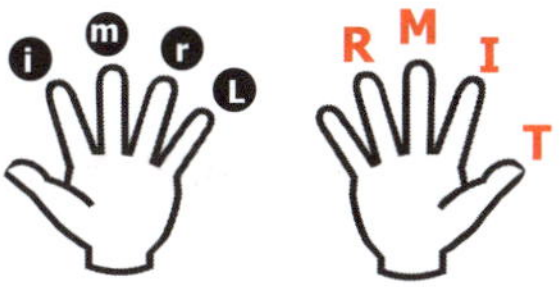

FP order: **T, I, M, R, M, I**

(Play each pattern twice)

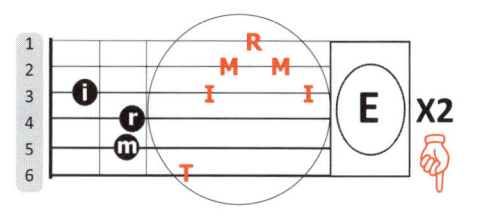

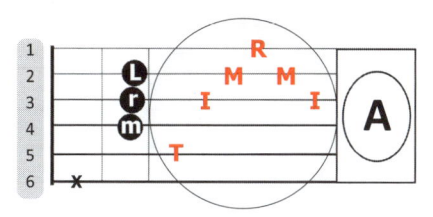

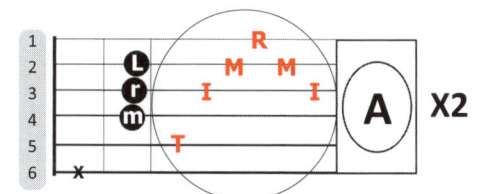

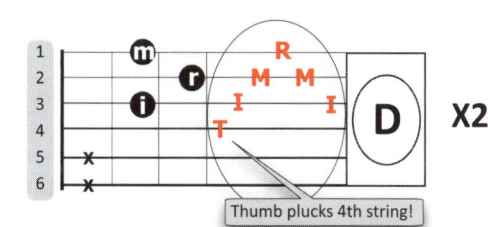

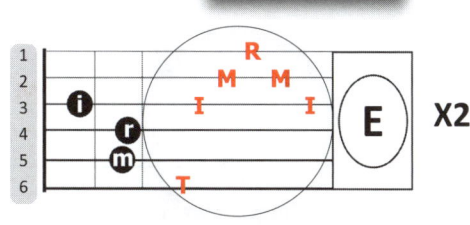

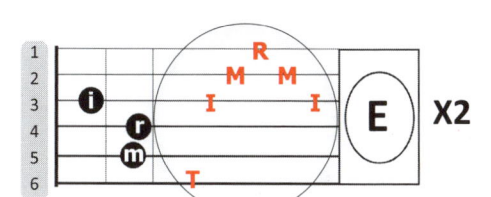

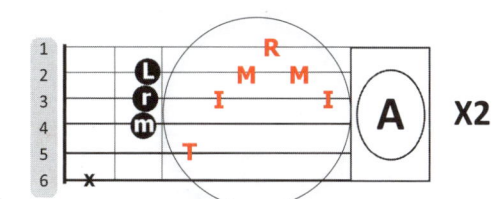

E X2

A X2

A X2

D X2 — Thumb plucks 4th string!

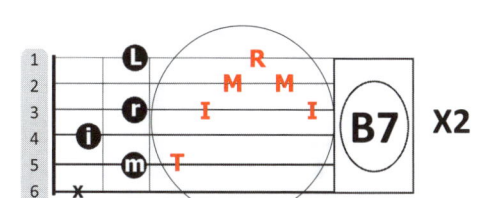

B7 X2

E X2

E X2

A X2

L7 target time: under 1 minute

DATE:					
TIME:					

L7 check: ☐ ☐ ☐

Ch4 L8 Finger picking

Finger picking lesson 8: FP the 16 CB: E, A, B7, D, G, and C

For this lesson we have 16 chords to finger pick. (Finger pick each pattern twice)

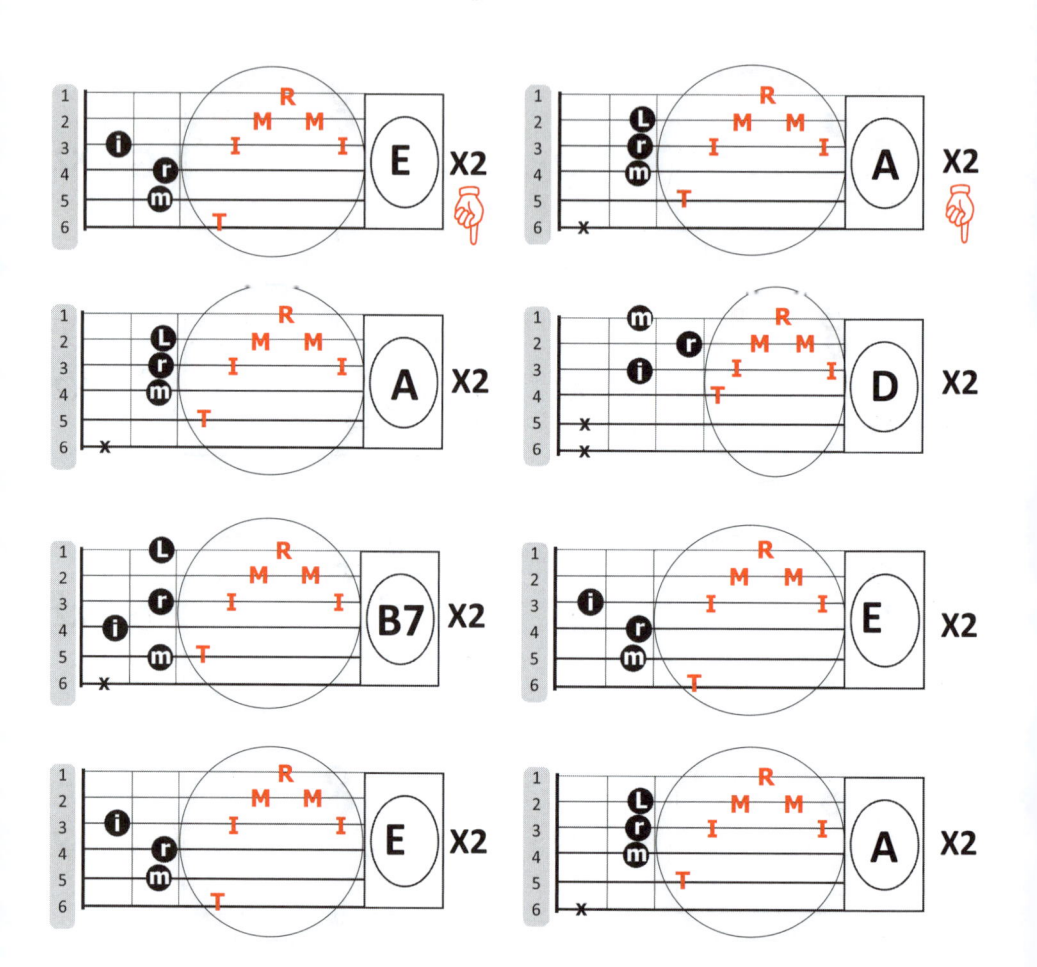

Finger picking **Ch4 L8**

- D X2
- G X2
- G X2
- C X2
- A X2
- D X2
- D X2
- G X2

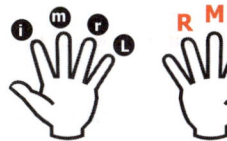

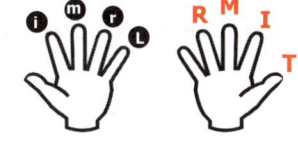

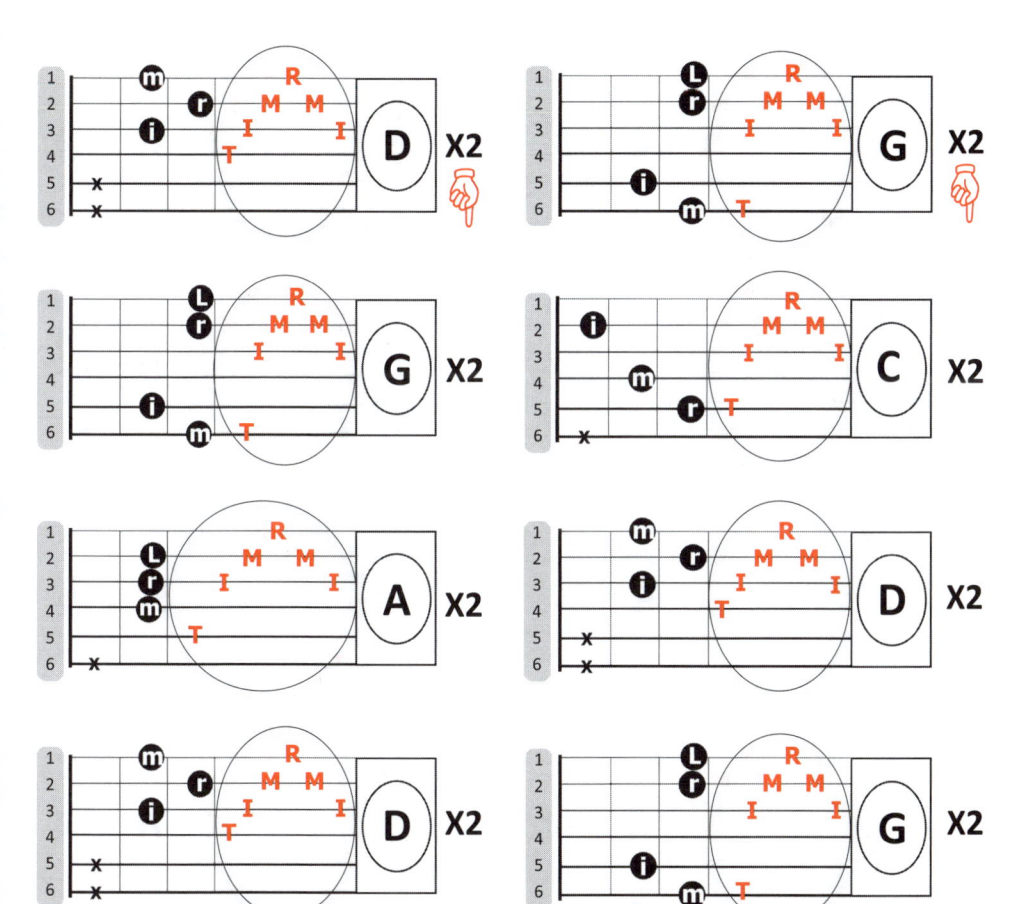

Top Tip

Lesson 8 goal: While maintaining the quality (i.e. don't rush!) finger pick each chord twice in under one minute, as smoothly as possible.

Don't worry if you are well outside this target time to begin with. Persevere with the flow and quality, and the speed will develop naturally over time.

L8 target time: under 1 minute

DATE:					
TIME:					

L8 check: ☐ ☐ ☐

Ch4 L9 Finger picking

Finger picking lesson 9: The 16 Chord Block without chord boxes

For this finger picking lesson we do exactly the same as lesson 8, but across the page in rows. The goal is to rely less on the chord diagrams and FP patterns, and commit to memory.

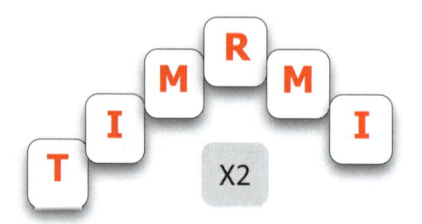

T-I-M-R-M-I (X2)

E	A	B7	E
A	D	E	A
D	G	A	D
G	C	D	G

L9 target time: under 1 minute

DATE:						
TIME:						

L9 check: ☐ ☐ ☐

Finger picking lesson 10: The 16 CB alternative finger picking patterns

Once you're confident with changing between chords, we can now try different finger picking patterns. Different patterns add variety and dynamics to your playing. The goal for this last lesson is to play all four finger picking patterns smoothly and evenly – in under four minutes.

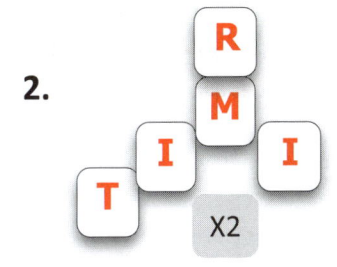

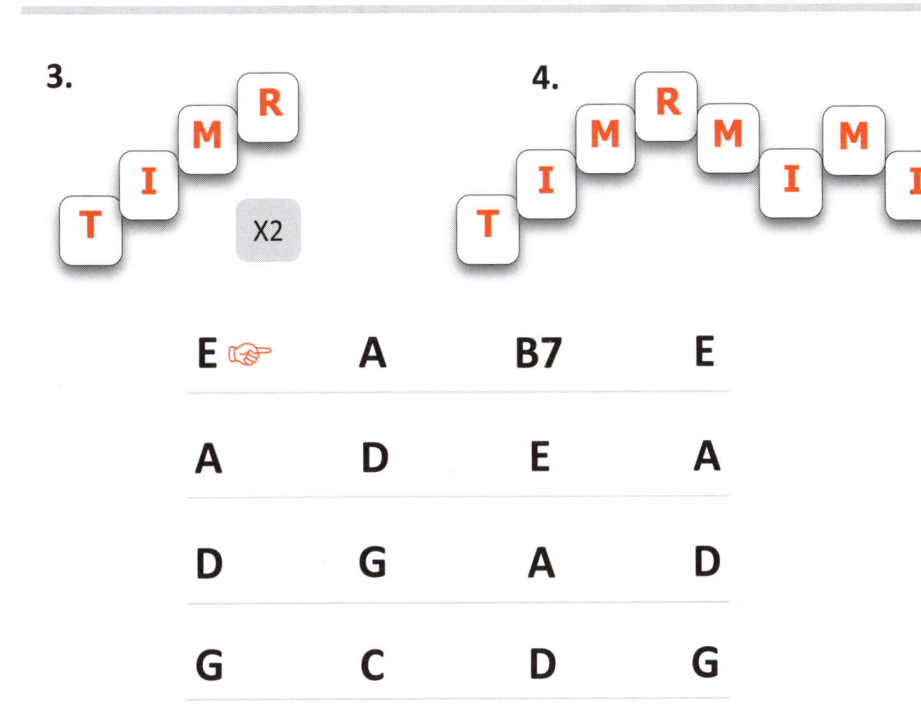

1. T I M R M I X2

2. T I M R M I X2

3. T I M R X2

4. T I M R M I M I

E ☞	A	B7	E
A	D	E	A
D	G	A	D
G	C	D	G

L10 target time: under 4 minutes

DATE:					
TIME:					

L10 check: ☐ ☐ ☐

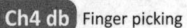

Finger picking debrief

Good work reaching this point – even if you're achieving lesson 10 between four and six minutes. It's all about repetition; the more you go over and over the 16 chord block, the smoother it will sound, and you will find your time getting quicker without realising it.

Practice does not need to be dull and repetitive. Although the nature of repeated exercise is a vital part of the process of mastering this skill, take it as a given and press on. Put the timer on for ten minutes, and just do it. Feel free to be creative if the mood takes you!

Finger picking is fiddly. It will feel awkward to begin with, but as you focus on the basic level 9 style, and just finger pick for ten minutes a day, I guarantee you will see a dramatic difference in your playing within three weeks.

Remember this is not a lifetime slog; the first few weeks and months may be a challenge in perseverance, but the rewards are so worth it. I repeat; you may feel like a slave to this instrument right now, but with practice you will become the master!

5 Understanding Classical Notation

In this chapter we shall be learning basic classical notation for the guitar.

Classical notation is a universal musical language that indicates rhythm, timing, and much more. Although for many it is harder to understand than TAB (which is limited to guitarists only, and does not indicate correct timing or rhythm), once classical notation is understood, it can be read by any musician on any instrument – anywhere in the world!

Page

CN lesson 1: Open strings, the rest stroke, crotchets and minims 62

CN lesson 2: The stave, and songs with the notes of E, B, and G 66

CN lesson 3: The dotted minim, semibreve, and the notes F and 'higher' G 70

CN lesson 4: Songs using the notes of B, C, and D 74

CN lesson 5: The major scales of G and C 78

For each song there are three self-evaluation squares that help you chart your own progress.

- ☑ (I've attempted this song a few times)
- ☑ ☑ (I'm definitely seeing progress on this song)
- ☑ ☑ ☑ (I can play this song quite smoothly and confidently)

Ch5 L1

Classical notation lesson 1: Open strings, the rest stroke, crotchets and minims

We're going to start off this lesson by learning the open string names and how to play the rest stroke. The open strings are just the strings played on their own without any fingers on the fret board. The rest stroke is the easiest way to produce a strong sounding note.

Open string notes

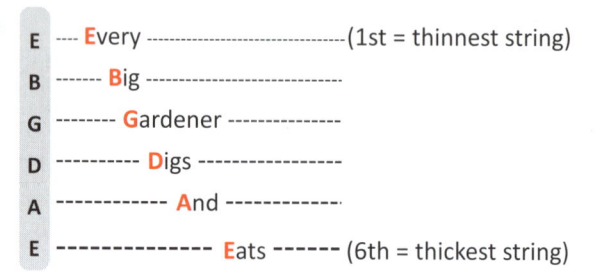

E ---- **E**very --------------------------------(1st = thinnest string)
B ------- **B**ig ----------------------------
G -------- **G**ardener ----------------
D ---------- **D**igs -----------------
A ------------- **A**nd -------------
E --------------- **E**ats ------ (6th = thickest string)

The rest stroke

1. Place your right hand thumb on the top string (6th)...

2. Place your straight index finger on the 1st string...

3. Pull (pluck) the string towards you...

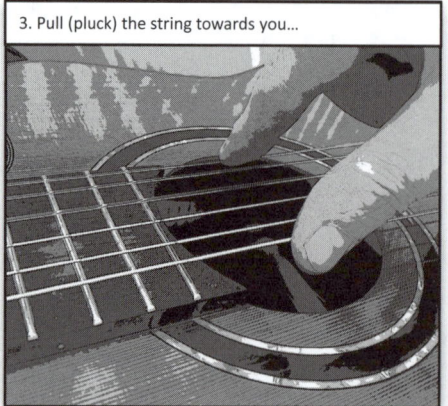

4. ...coming to 'rest' on the string above.

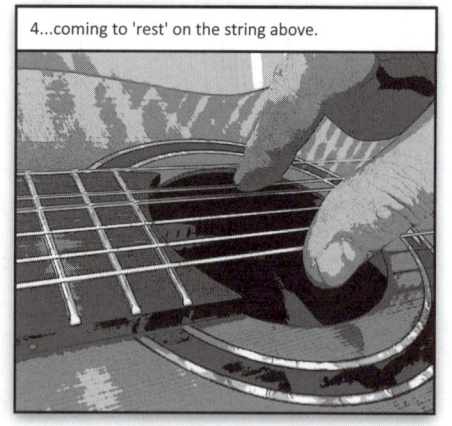

Ch5 L1

The Crotchet

This note is called a crotchet – each note lasts for one beat.*

1. Use the rest stroke technique to pluck the 1st string (E) four times.

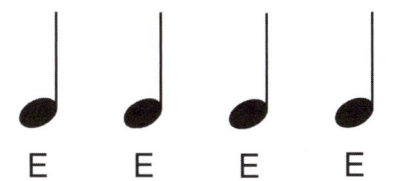

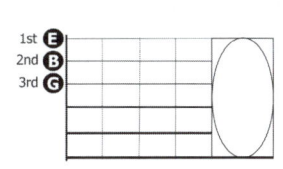

E   E   E   E

1st **E**
2nd **B**
3rd **G**

2. Now pluck the 2nd string (B) slowly and evenly x8.

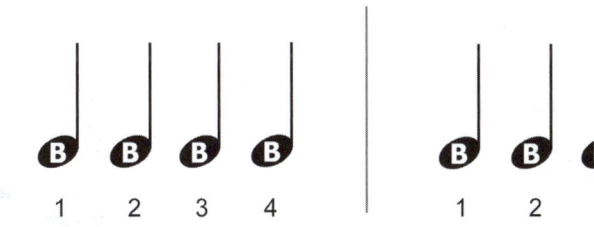

B   B   B   B | B   B   B   B
1   2   3   4   1   2   3   4

3. Now try and mixture of E, B, and the new note of G (3rd string).

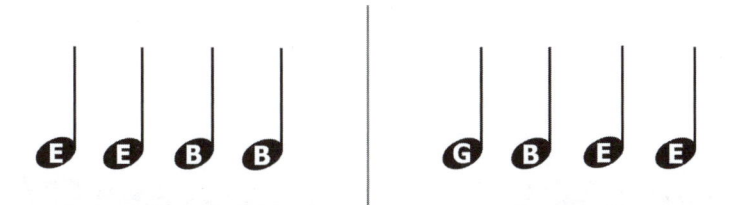

E   E   B   B | G   B   E   E

* A crotchet lasts for one beat in the most common time signatures of 4/4, and 3/4.

Top Tip The tempo is the speed of a song – play one note every second and this would be 60 BPM (beats per minute). It might help to count aloud as you play 1,2,3,4 etc.

Ch5 L1

The minim

This note is called a minim — each note lasts for two beats.

Now pluck the 1st string (E) four times.
As you play each note, try counting '1...2...' out loud to help you keep time.

1.

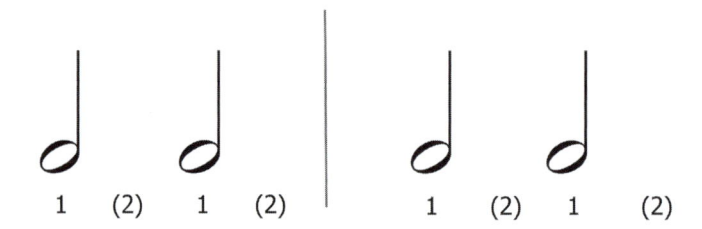

1 (2) 1 (2) | 1 (2) 1 (2)

♩ = 1 beat (crotchet)
𝅗𝅥 = 2 beats (minim)

Try these two exercises using the 1st string (E).

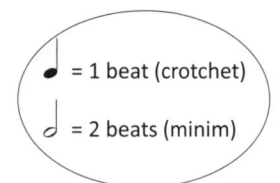

2. "Feel the Beat"

3. "Feel the Beat 2"

Ch5 L1

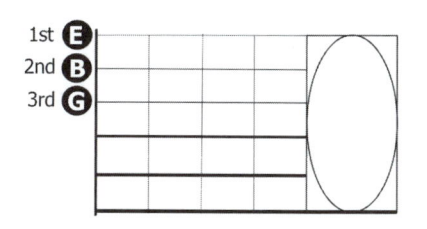

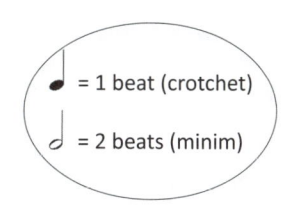

♩ = 1 beat (crotchet)
𝅗𝅥 = 2 beats (minim)

Now let's use the 1st, 2nd and 3rd string (E, B, and G).

1. "Up and Down"

Count in: 1,2,3,4... (see Top Tip below).

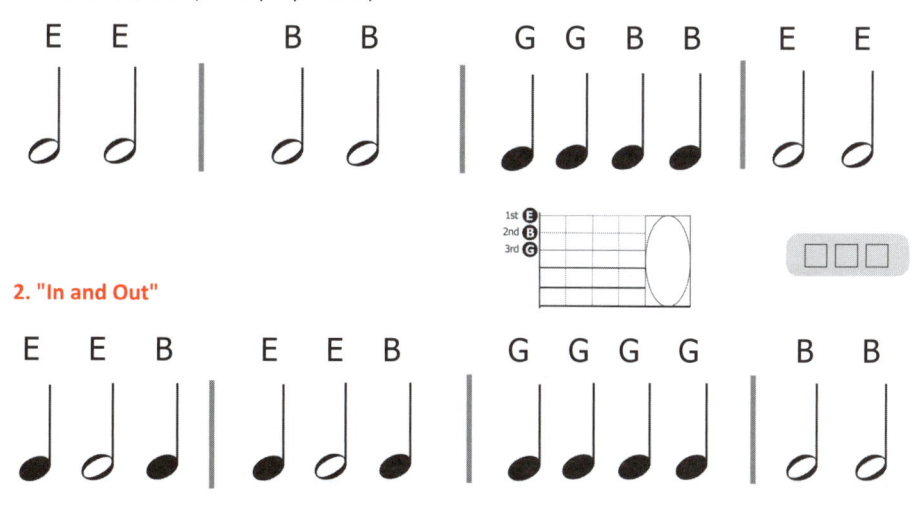

E E | B B | G G B B | E E

2. "In and Out"

E E B | E E B | G G G G | B B

> **Top Tip**
> As you play these last couple of exercises from lesson 1, try 'counting in' before you start playing. A 'count in' or 'count off' is a verbal cue for you (and others if you play in a group or band) as to the tempo of the song. For most songs it will simply be 1, 2, 3, 4... and then begin.

Ch5 L2 ♩

Classical notation lesson 2: The stave, and songs with the notes of E, B, and G

Musical notes (like crotchets and minims) are written on a five line stave.

Notes sit either **on** the lines, or **in** the spaces between the lines.

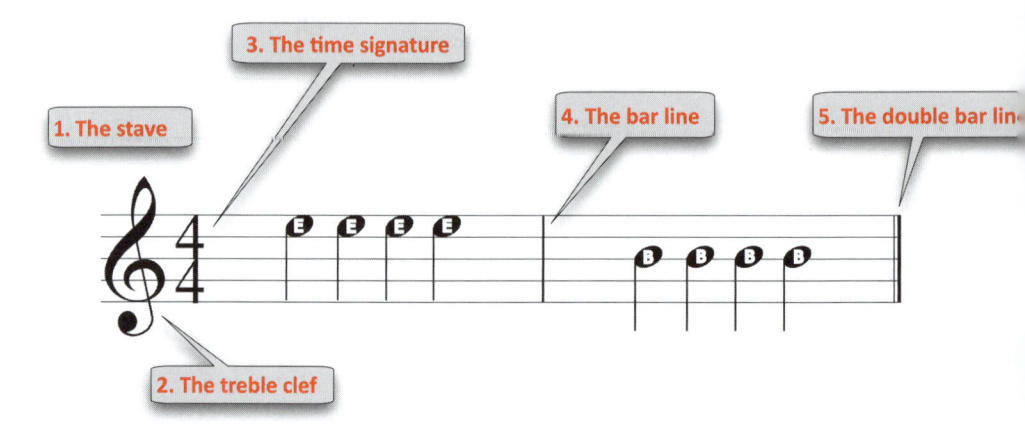

- 1. The stave
- 2. The treble clef
- 3. The time signature
- 4. The bar line
- 5. The double bar line

1. The stave is a group of five lines on which music is written.

2. The treble clef symbol* tells you that the notes on this stave are from the upper half of the piano (treble notes).

3. The time signature '4/4' shows that there are four beats in a bar. That means that all the notes within the bar have to add up to four.

4. The bar line shows the end of one bar, and the beginning of another.

5. The double bar line is used to show the very end of the music.

* This squiggly treble clef symbol is actually a stylized letter 'G' that encircles the 2nd line of the stave indicated that line to be G above middle C.

Top Tip

Note stems:
If a note head is on or above the middle line of the stave, its stem points down.
If the note head is below the middle line of the stave, its stem points up. This is mainly to make things look neat and tidy on the page.

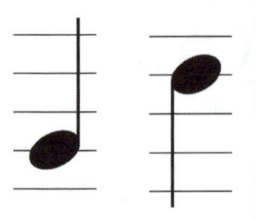

Ch5 L2

Let's get to know where the open **1st and 2nd strings** (E and B) are on the stave.

Play each song slowly and carefully giving each note the correct duration.

You may find it helpful to count through each bar aloud as you play 1,2,3,4 etc.

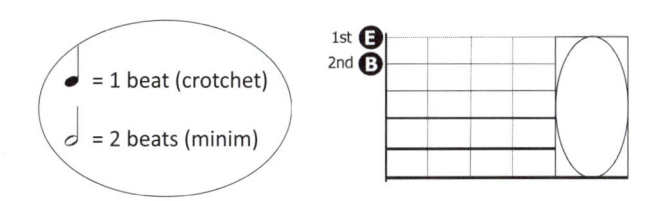

♩ = 1 beat (crotchet)

𝅗𝅥 = 2 beats (minim)

1st **E**
2nd **B**

1. "The E Tune" (1st string, E)

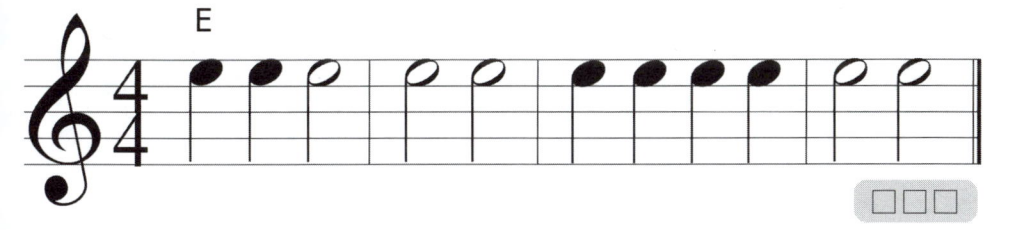

2. "The B Tune" (2nd string, B)

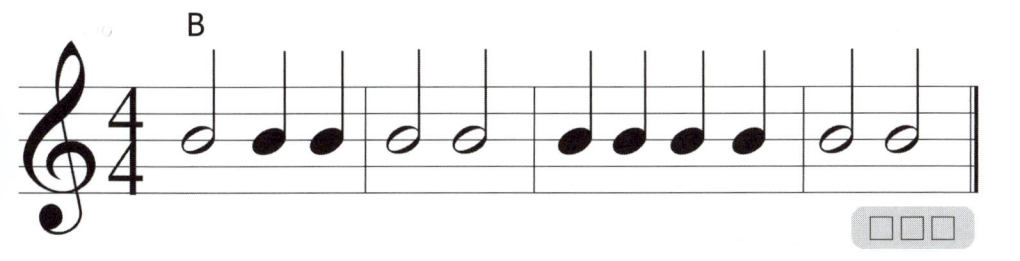

3. "E Against B" (1st/2nd string, E and B)

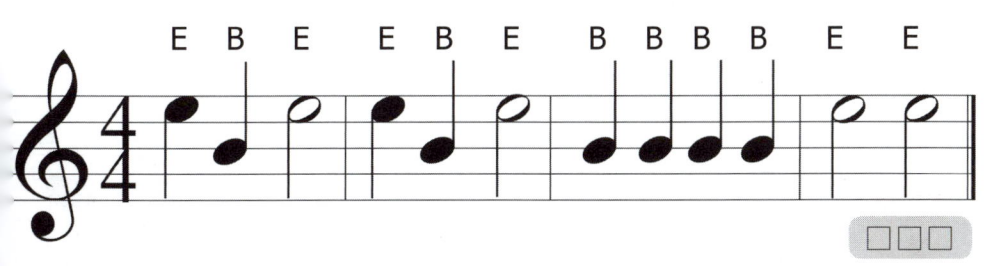

Watch the videos
www.loveguitar.co.uk

Ch5 L2

This is where the open **3rd string** (G) is on the stave.

The songs on this page can be played on their own, or together as a duet or trio.

Remember: try and keep to the 60 bpm (beats per minute) tempo – one note every second.

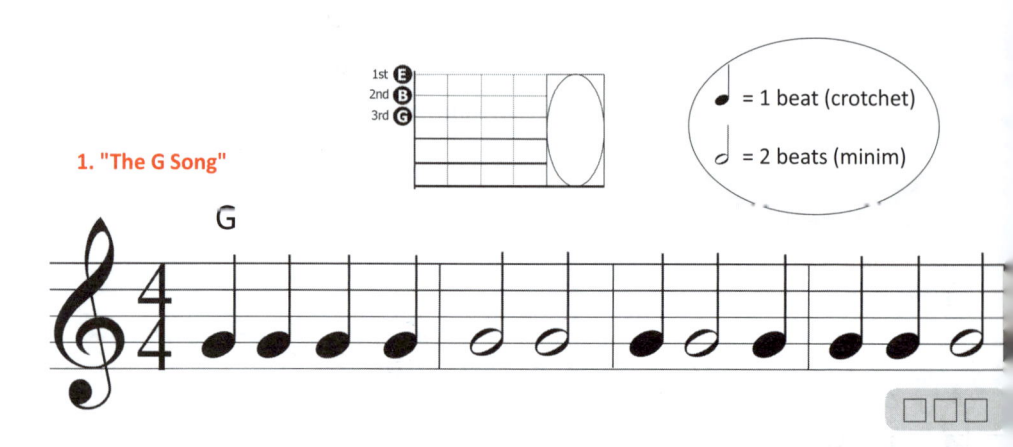

♩ = 1 beat (crotchet)

𝅗𝅥 = 2 beats (minim)

1. "The G Song"

2. "Three in a Boat"

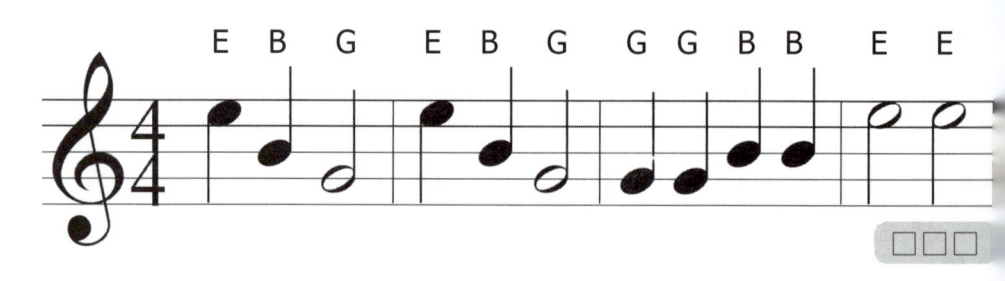

3. "Two in a Boat"

Don't use rest stroke for this song but pluck the **1st and 2nd strings** together using your RH index finger (B) and middle finger (E)

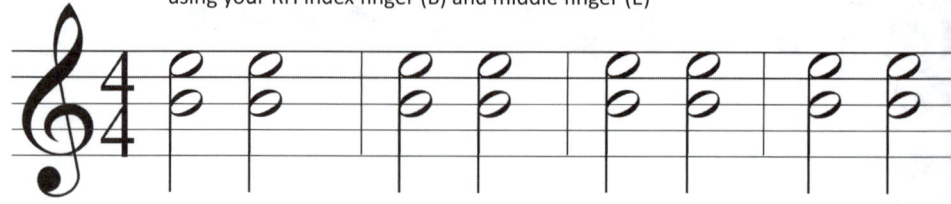

68

Ch5 L2

Let's learn a couple more songs using the **1st, 2nd and 3rd open strings** (E, B and G).

If you know anyone else who can play guitar, these also sound great played together as a duet.

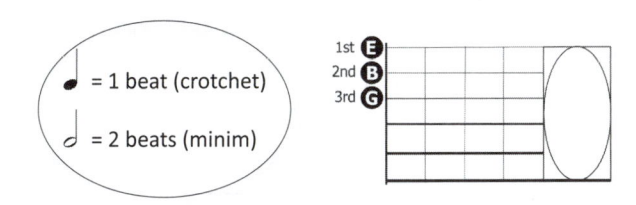

♩ = 1 beat (crotchet)

𝅗𝅥 = 2 beats (minim)

1st **E**
2nd **B**
3rd **G**

1. "Going to Sleep"

(Using the 1st, 2nd and 3rd string)

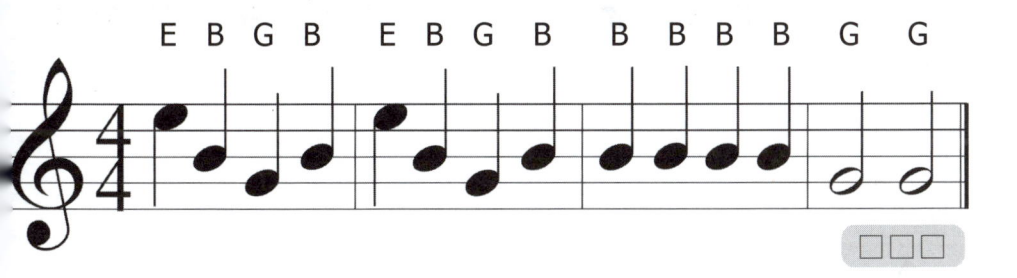

E B G B | E B G B | B B B B | G G

2. "Waking Up"

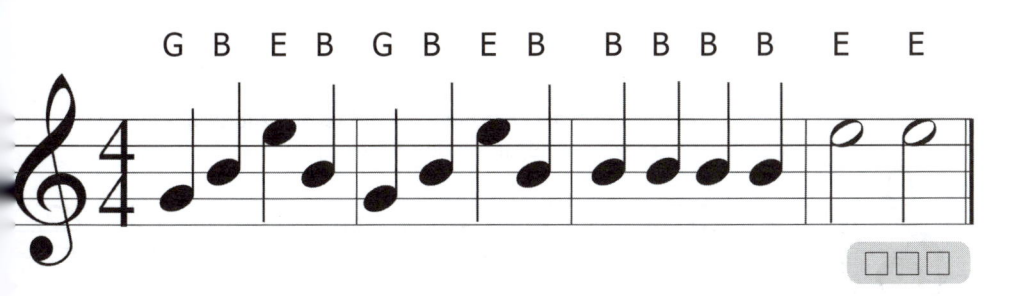

G B E B | G B E B | B B B B | E E

Classical notation lesson 3: The dotted minim, semibreve, and the notes F and 'higher' C

The dotted minim

This note is called a dotted minim – each note lasts for 3 beats.

Now pluck the 1st string (E) four times.

As you play each note, try counting '1...2...3...' out loud to help you keep time.

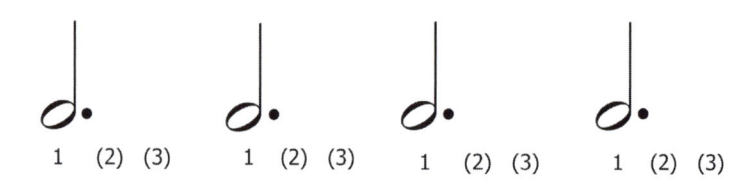

| 1 (2) (3) | 1 (2) (3) | 1 (2) (3) | 1 (2) (3) |

The semibreve

This note is called a semibreve – each note lasts for 4 beats.

Now pluck the 1st string (E) four times.

As you play each note, try counting '1...2...3...4...' out loud to help you keep time.

| 1 (2, 3, 4) | 1 (2, 3, 4) | 1 (2, 3, 4) | 1 (2, 3, 4) |

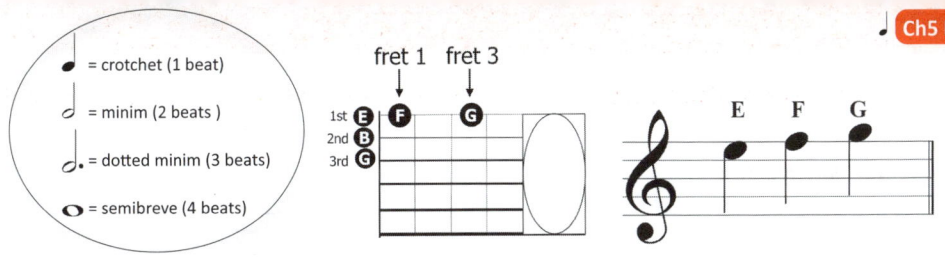

♩ Ch5 L3

♩ = crotchet (1 beat)
𝅗𝅥 = minim (2 beats)
𝅗𝅥. = dotted minim (3 beats)
𝅝 = semibreve (4 beats)

fret 1 fret 3
1st E F
2nd B
3rd G

E F G

In the next few songs, we're going to use everything we've learnt so far:

• the **1st, 2nd, and 3rd string** (E, B, and G), **crotchets** (1 beat), **minims** (2 beats), **dotted minims** (3 beats), **semibreves** (4 beats) – and introduce the notes **F and 'higher' G**.

G and 'higher' G – both notes are called G but are an octave apart (an octave is an interval of 8 notes) – 'higher' G is an octave above the previous G introduced on p68.

1. "Lazy Gee"

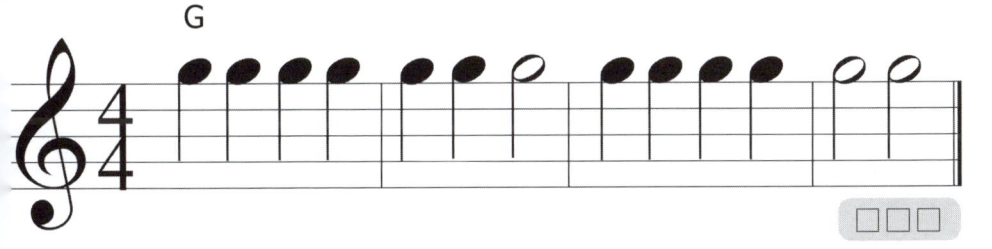

G

2. "Low Lazy Gee"

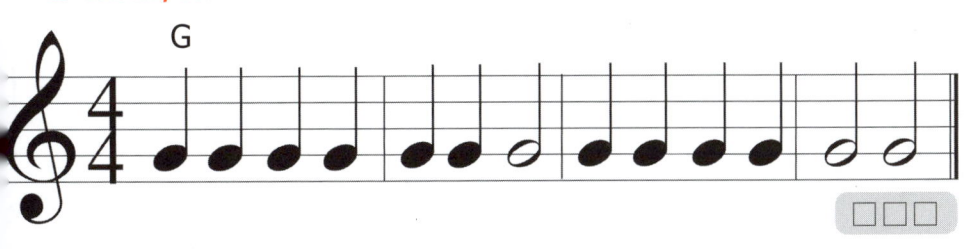

G

3. "High and Low"

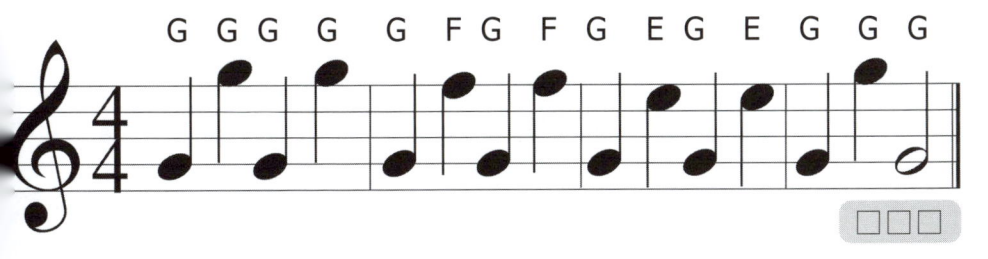

G G G G G F G F G E G E G G

71

Ch5 L3 ♩

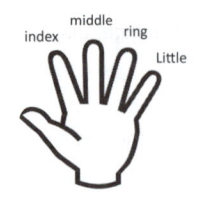

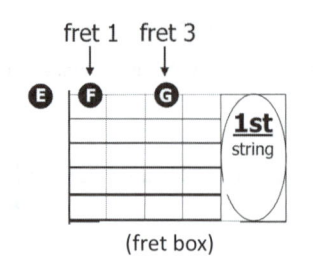

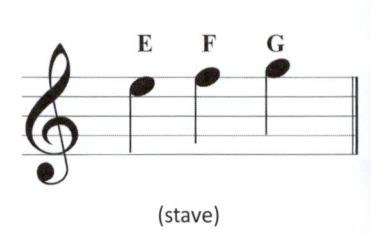

(fret box)   (stave)

Pluck using your left hand index finger for the F note, and the ring for the 'higher' G note.

These songs can be played on their own, or in a duet or trio.

1. "Skimming Stones" (part 1)

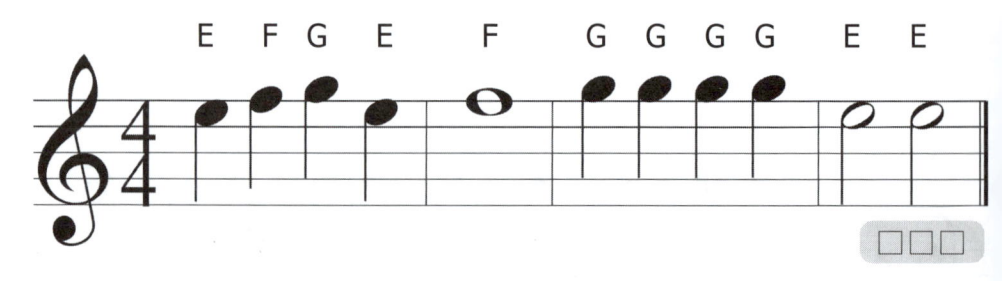

E F G E   F   G G G G   E E

2. "Skimming Stones" (part 2)

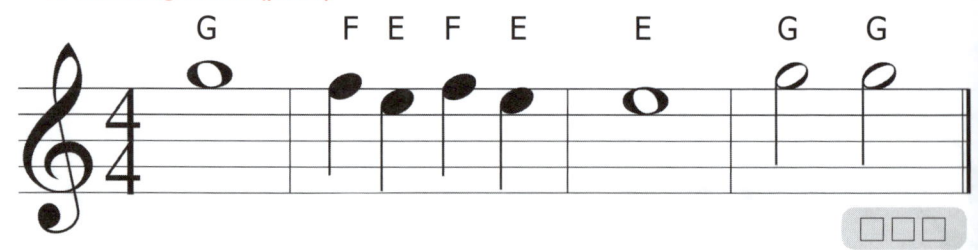

G   F E F E   E   G G

3. "Skimming Stones" (part 3)

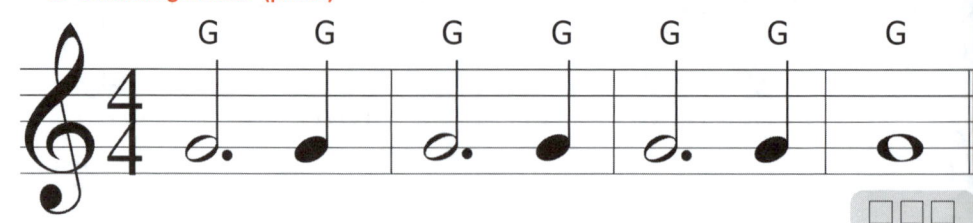

G G G G G G G

Ch5 L3

Use your right hand thumb to play the open **3rd string** (G) while your RH Index finger plays the **1st string** at the same time.

On the fretboard use your left hand index finger for the F note, and the ring for the G note.

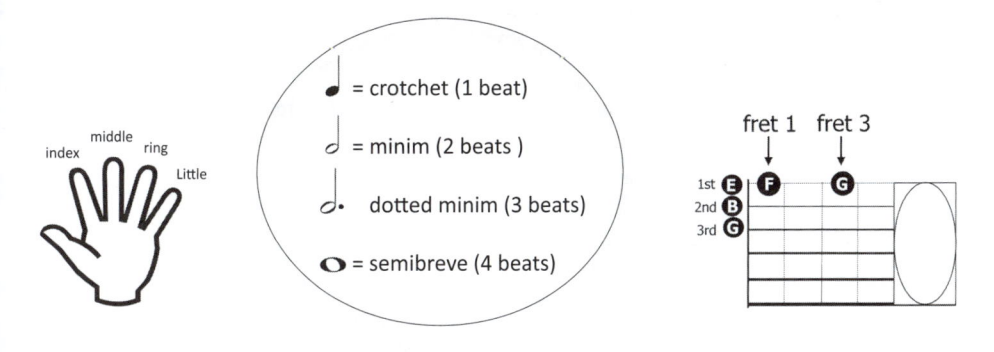

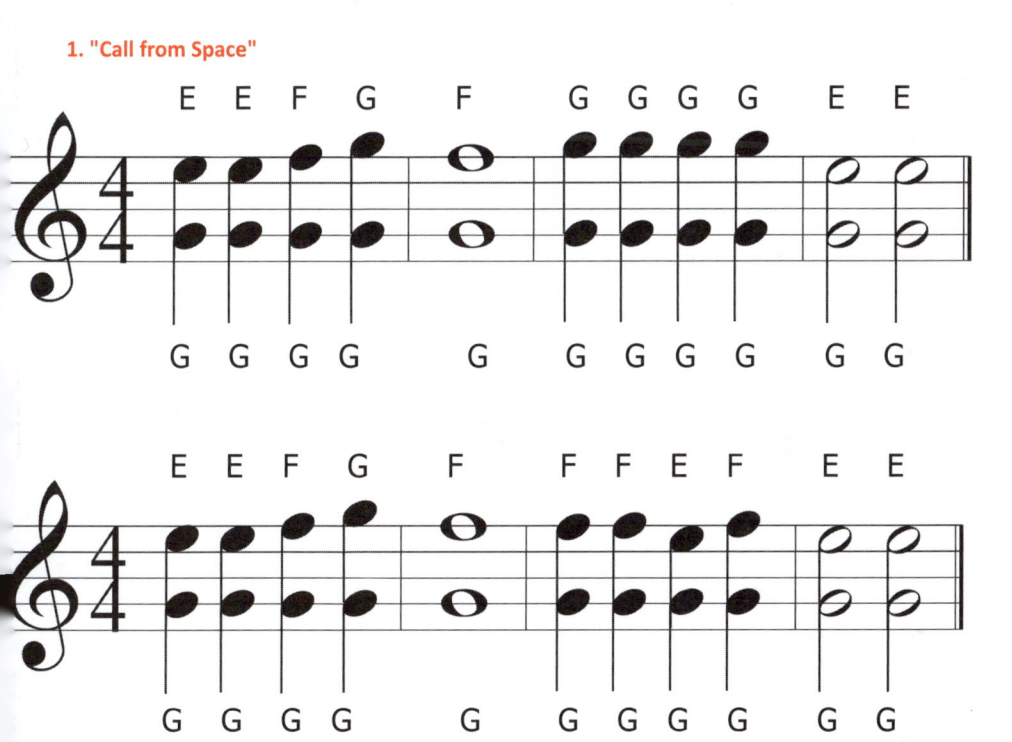

♩ = crotchet (1 beat)

𝅗𝅥 = minim (2 beats)

𝅗𝅥. dotted minim (3 beats)

𝅝 = semibreve (4 beats)

1. "Call from Space"

Classical notation lesson 4: Songs using the notes B, C, and D

Let's now look at the notes of B, C, and D.

B is the open string (2nd) while the notes C and D will be played using the index and ring finger (left hand).

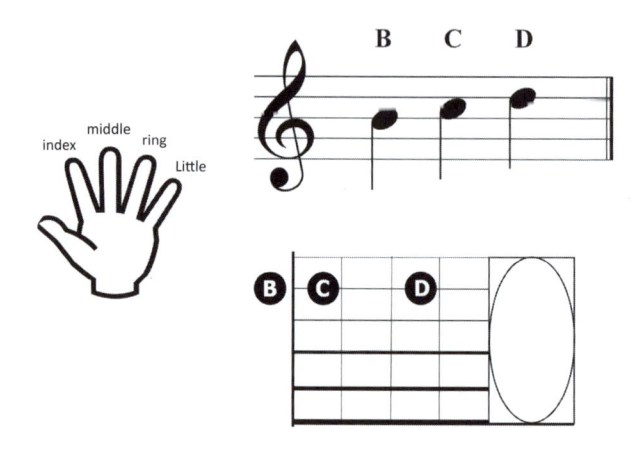

"Ball Around Bee"

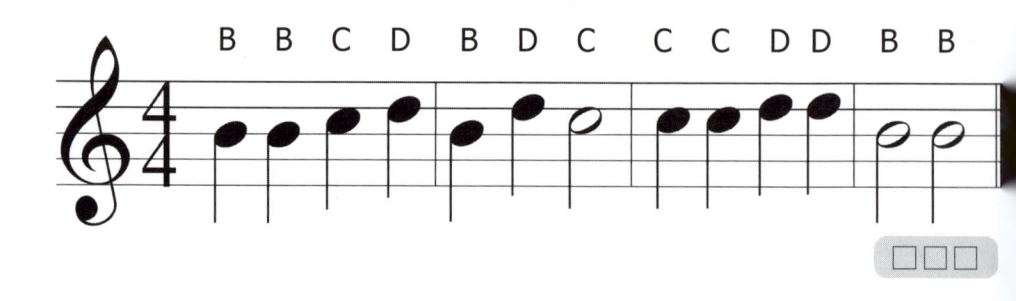

B B C D B D C C C D D B B

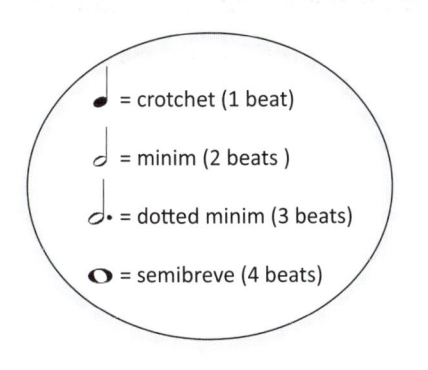

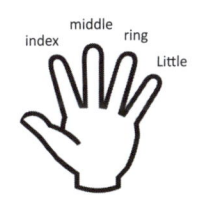

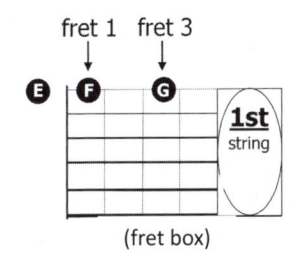

Ch5 L4

♩ = crotchet (1 beat)
𝅗𝅥 = minim (2 beats)
𝅗𝅥. = dotted minim (3 beats)
𝅝 = semibreve (4 beats)

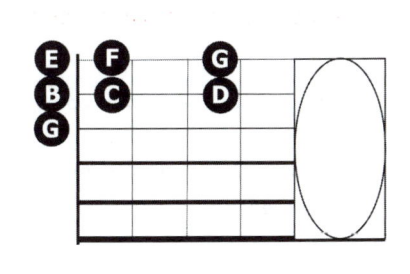

(fret box)

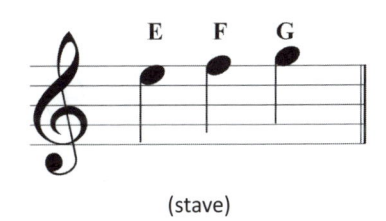

(stave)

1. "Small Steps" (part 1)

Count in: 1,2,3,4...

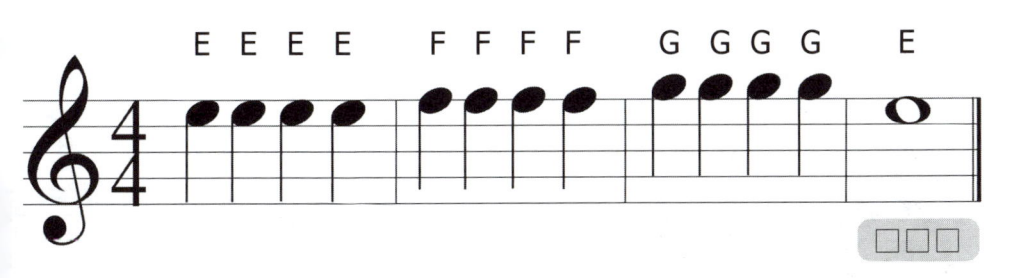

E E E E   F F F F   G G G G   E

2. "Small Steps" (part 2)

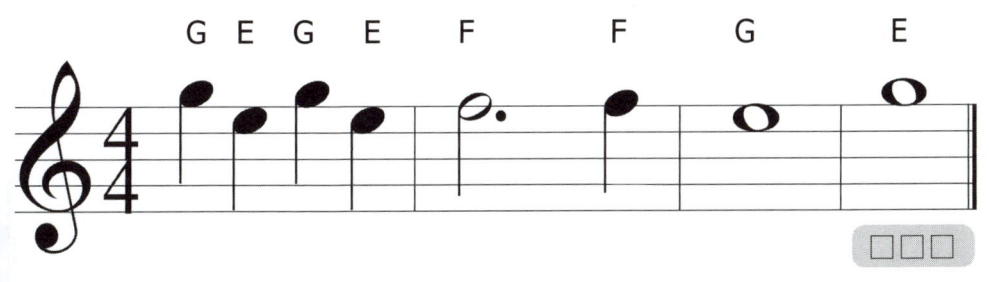

G E G E   F   F   G   E

75

Ch5 L4

Try these songs – they will sound great whether you play them on their own, choose two to play in a duet, or play all three as a trio.

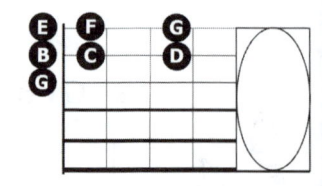

1. "Saints Away" (pt 1)

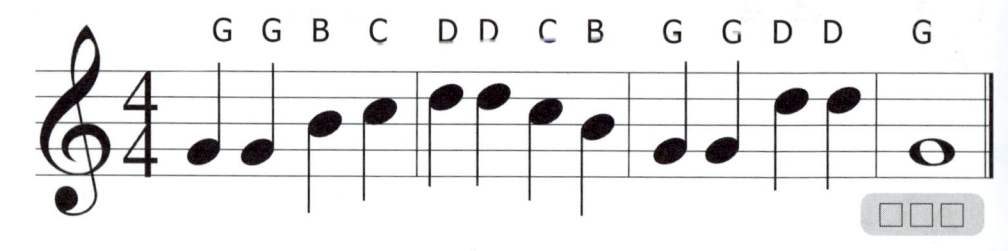

G G B C D D C B G G D D G

2. "Saints Away" (pt 2)

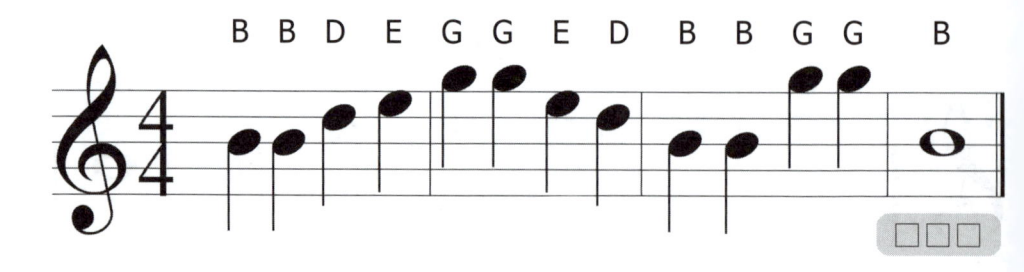

B B D E G G E D B B G G B

3. "Saints Away" (pt 3)

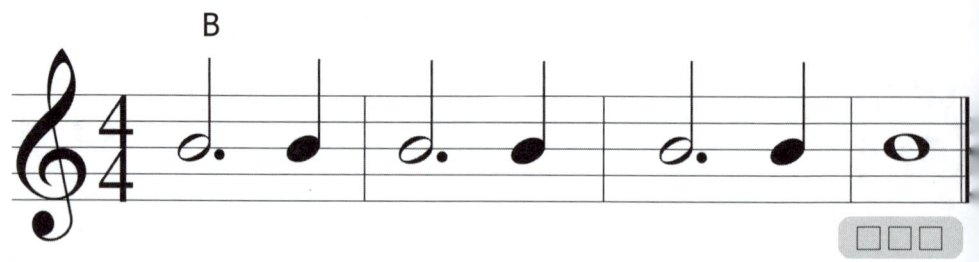

B

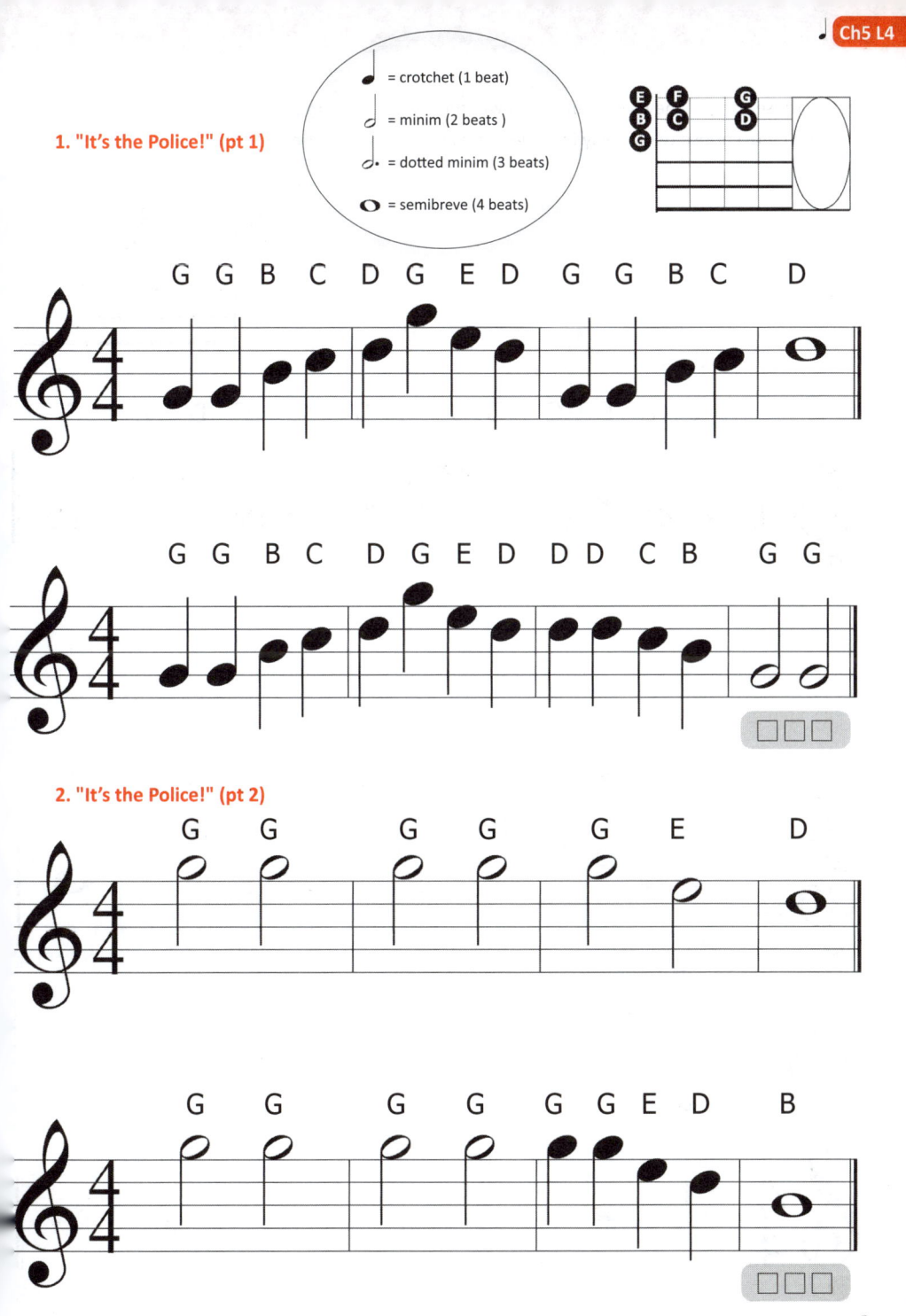

Ch5 L4

♩ = crotchet (1 beat)
𝅗𝅥 = minim (2 beats)
𝅗𝅥. = dotted minim (3 beats)
𝅝 = semibreve (4 beats)

1. "It's the Police!" (pt 1)

G G B C D G E D G G B C D

G G B C D G E D D D C B G G

2. "It's the Police!" (pt 2)

G G G G G E D

G G G G G G E D B

Classical notation level 5: The major scales of C and G

For this last lesson we'll be looking at the major scales of C and G.

These are the fretboard notes for the C major scale (up to G).

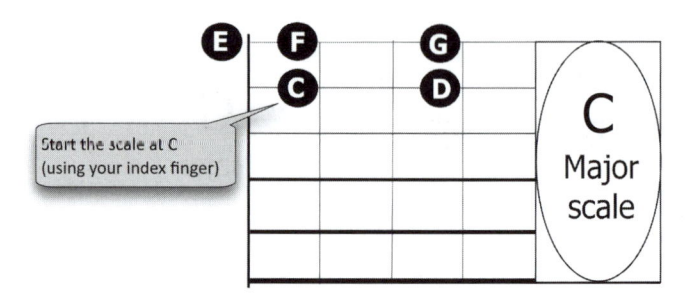

Start the scale at C (using your index finger)

C Major scale

And this is what it looks like on the stave...

C major scale (to G)

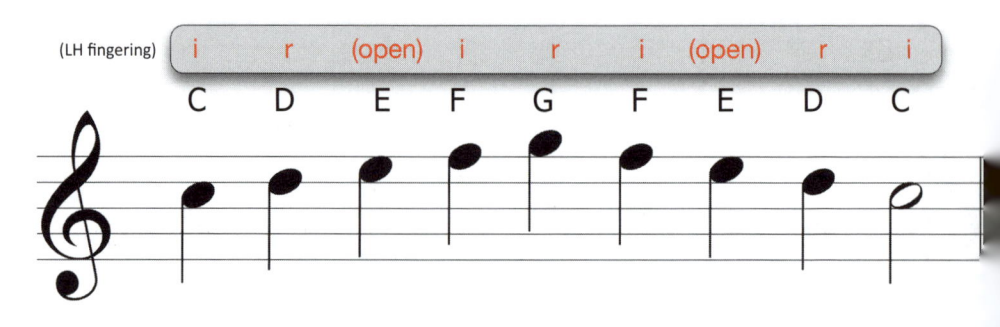

(LH fingering) i   r   (open)   i   r   i   (open)   r   i
                C   D   E   F   G   F   E   D   C

These are the fretboard notes for the G major scale (up to D).

Look out for the new note of A (3rd string, 2nd fret).

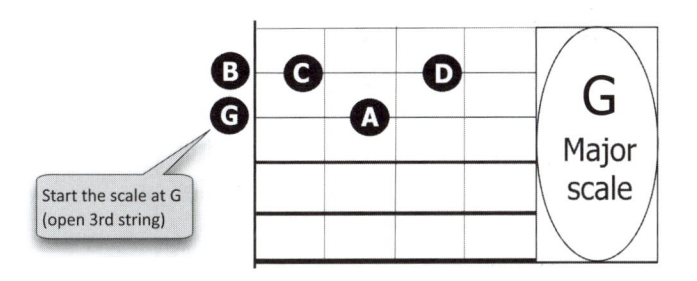

G Major scale

Start the scale at G (open 3rd string)

And this is what it looks like on the stave...

G major scale (to D)

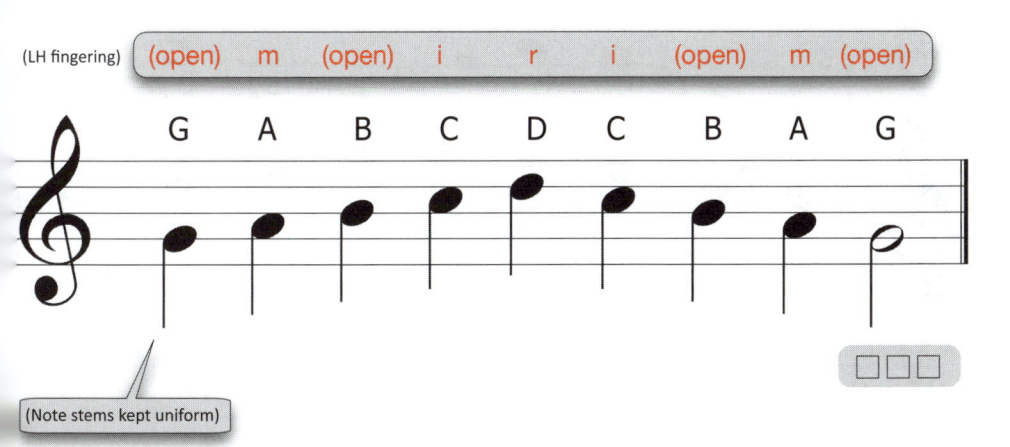

(LH fingering) (open) m (open) i r i (open) m (open)

G A B C D C B A G

(Note stems kept uniform)

Watch the videos
www.loveguitar.co.uk

Ch5 L5

These songs are good for solo playing or in a duet.

♩ = crotchet (1 beat)
𝅗𝅥 = minim (2 beats)
𝅗𝅥. = dotted minim (3 beats)
𝅝 = semibreve (4 beats)

1. "C in 5" (pt 1)

C D E F G F E D C G C

: Repeat sign

2. "C in 5" (pt 2)

C G C D E F G

3. "G in 5" (pt 1)

C D E F G F E D C G C

4. "G in 5" (pt 2)

C G C D E F G

Guitar Note Finder™

Ch5 L5

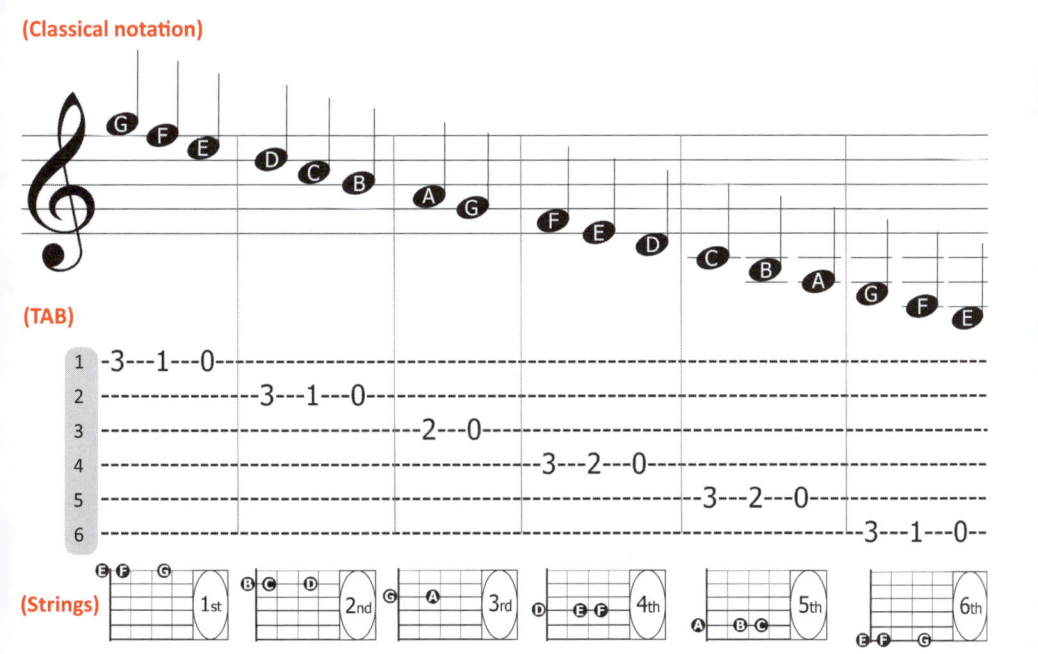

(Classical notation)

(TAB)

```
1 -3---1--0----------------------------------------------------------
2 -----------3---1--0-------------------------------------------------
3 -------------------2--0---------------------------------------------
4 -------------------------3---2--0-----------------------------------
5 -----------------------------------3---2--0-------------------------
6 -----------------------------------------------3---1--0-------------
```

(Strings)

1st: E F G
2nd: B C D
3rd: G A
4th: D E F
5th: A B C
6th: E F G

Classical notation debrief

Learning classical notation on the guitar takes perseverance and clear focus, so good work on getting this far!

It's really about knowing the notes on the stave in relation to the notes on the fretboard – or if it's easier, knowing the notes on the fretboard in relation to the stave.

A good starting point is becoming familiar with the notes on the guitar note finder.

Remember, this chapter just gives the simplest introduction to notation. If you want to explore classical guitar in greater depth I recommend Richard Corr's excellent *Guitar Academy* method – *www.guitaracademy.co.uk*.
Alternatively you can always borrow a keyboard and check out John Thompson's *Easiest Piano Course* to get an understanding of notation from that particular route.

Back of the Book
Extras

6

So, you've been learning the guitar for a few months, got the six basic chords off by heart, strummed a few songs, but you need a little more challenge. This section has been written to give you a nudge in the right direction – a springboard to the next stage of your journey. Take a look at some Tommy Emmanuel videos and you will quickly realise in some ways the rest of us are beginners! But how do you judge your own performance? How can you tell when you are moving from 'beginner' to 'intermediate'?

We are all driven to get better in different ways, and for different reasons. Safe to say we all want to improve from where we are now. When I started learning, my goal was to be confident on my instrument, to enjoy playing and singing without needing to look at my fingers – for the guitar to be a kind of seamless expression of the inner sounds and rhythms I enjoyed (and still enjoy) most.

So I have put together ten 'back of the book extras' that incorporate all the things I would have appreciated working on after my initial six months of learning. Enjoy!

Page

Extras lesson 1: Scales 84

Extras lesson 2: Six must-know minor chords 87

Extras lesson 3: Full-bar chord shapes 88

Extras lesson 4: Half-bar chord shapes 89

Extras lesson 5: Ten cool riffs 90

Extras lesson 6: Ten cool chord progressions 93

Extras lesson 7: "Minuet in G" 95

Extras lesson 8: "Greensleeves" 96

Extras lesson 9: Ten easy songs (using the chords of D, G, and A) 97

Extras lessons 10: Really useful chord page 102

Watch the videos
www.loveguitar.co.uk

Ch6 E1 Extras

Extras lesson 1: Scales

Scales are the bread and butter of good technique – ask any top classical concert performer. If you want to do one thing to improve above all other things, practise scales. Over and over. Tedious and boring it may be, but absolutely key to polished and confident playing.

This lesson will include the **FF scale**, the **major scale**, and the **blues scale**.

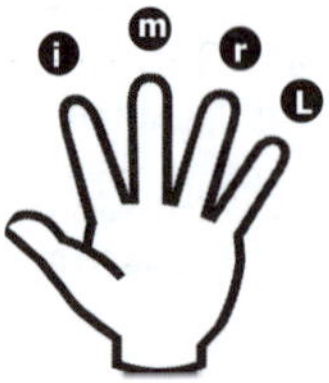

1. The FF scale (finger to a fret)

The FF scale (finger to a fret) is a simple yet very effective exercise. It strengthens the fingers and improves speed around the fretboard – your hand will be a similar shape as the left hand home position (p10).

Make good technique your highest priority. Keep the LH thumb upright, and make each note sound as clear as you can.

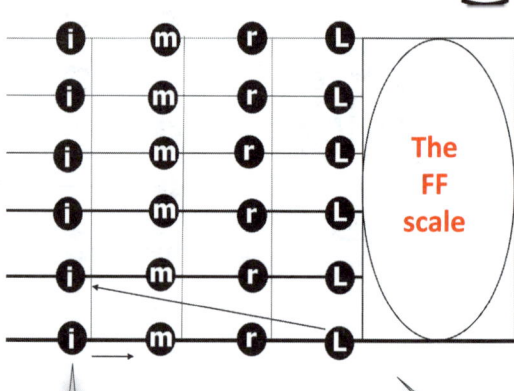

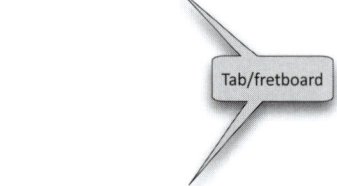

The FF scale

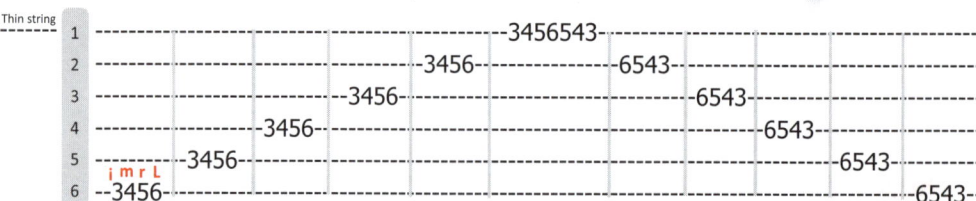

start here

Tab/fretboard

Top Tip
- fingertips
- pressing down
- just behind the fret

```
Thin string
         1 --------------------------------------3456543-------------------------------
         2 -----------------------------3456---------------6543-------------------------
         3 --------------------3456-----------------------------6543--------------------
         4 -----------3456-----------------------------------------------6543-----------
         5 ----3456---------------------------------------------------------------6543--
            i m r L
         6 -3456----------------------------------------------------------------------6543-
```

all 3's = use **i**ndex finger
all 4's = use **m**iddle finger
all 5's = use **r**ing finger
all 6's = use **L**ittle finger

Target times are only a guide; the first few times you attempt this might take you between one and two minutes to complete. The more times you try, the quicker you will get without even realising it. Try to keep a good technique (thumb behind neck/fingertips behind frets), and you'll see how the process of repetition will strengthen your fingers, and produce clearer sounding notes at the same time.

Target time: 20-30 seconds

DATE:					
TIME:					

Extras **Ch6 E1**

2. The major scale

```
n string
     1  ----------------------------|--------------|--i-2--m-3--|--i-2--------|-------------|-------------
     2  ----------------------------|--m-3--L-5----|------------|--L-5--m-3---|-------------|-------------
     3  ----------------------------|--i-2--r-4--L-5|-----------|--L-5--r-4--i-2|-----------|-------------
     4  --------------------|--i-2--r-4--L-5--|----|------------|-------L-5---|--r-4--i-2---|-------------
     5  ------|--i-2--m-3--L-5--|---|---------|----|------------|-------------|-------L-5---|--m-3--i-2---
     6  --m-3--L-5--|-----------|---|---------|----|------------|-------------|-------------|-------L-5---|--m-3--
```

(This scale is G major)

tab/fret board

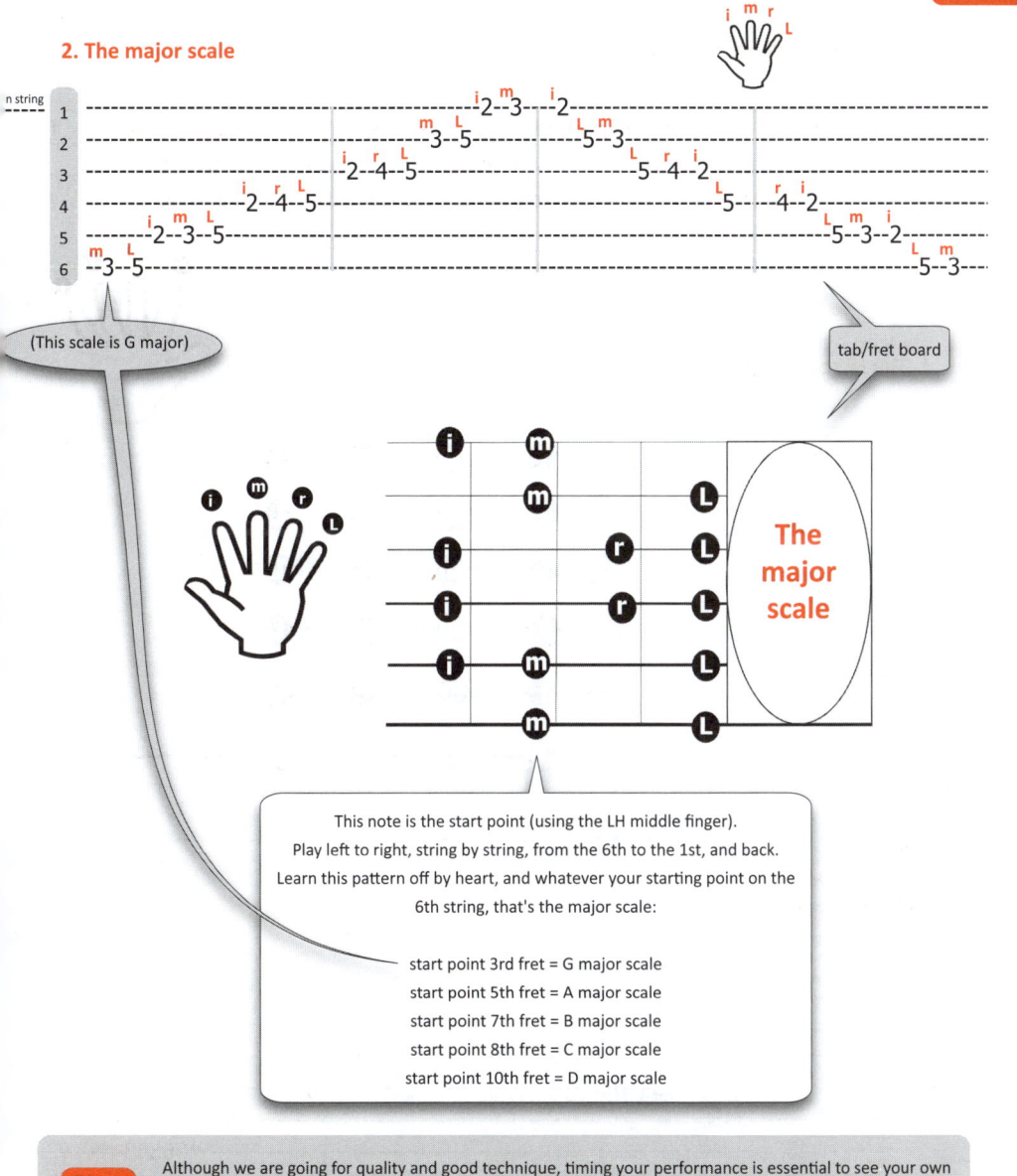

The major scale

This note is the start point (using the LH middle finger). Play left to right, string by string, from the 6th to the 1st, and back. Learn this pattern off by heart, and whatever your starting point on the 6th string, that's the major scale:

start point 3rd fret = G major scale
start point 5th fret = A major scale
start point 7th fret = B major scale
start point 8th fret = C major scale
start point 10th fret = D major scale

Top Tip Although we are going for quality and good technique, timing your performance is essential to see your own progress. Remember, this is not a speed test; you are merely seeing how long it takes you to play it as well as you can. Do this every day for two weeks, and with the simple process of repetition you will be amazed at your improvement.

Target time: 20-30 seconds

DATE:				
TIME:				

Ch6 E1 Extras

3. The blues scale

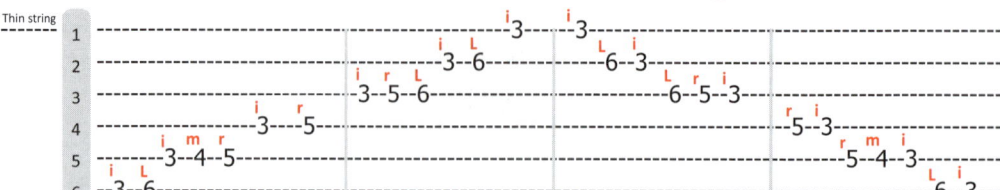

```
Thin string       i    i
  1 -------------------3-----3-------------------------------
            i   L            L  i
  2 ----------3--6-----------6--3----------------------------
         i  r  L                  L  r  i
  3 ----3--5--6----------------------6--5--3-----------------
      i     r                              r  i
  4 --3-----5--------------------------5--3------------------
    i  m  r                                  r  m  i
  5 -3--4--5-----------------------------5--4--3-------------
  i  L                                          L  i
  6 3--6-------------------------------------------6--3------
```

(As it starts on a G, this scale above is called the G blues scale)

All 3's = use **i**ndex finger
All 4's = use **m**iddle finger
All 5's = use **r**ing finger
All 6's = use **L**ittle finger

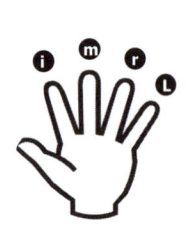

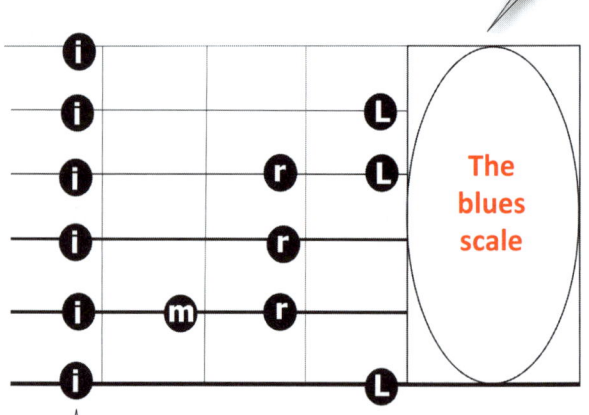

tab/fretboard

The blues scale

This note is the start point (using the LH index finger).
Play left to right, string by string, from the 6th to the 1st, and back.
Learn this pattern off by heart, and whatever your starting point on the
6th string, that's the blues scale key:

start point 3rd fret = G blues scale
start point 5th fret = A blues scale
start point 7th fret = B blues scale
start point 8th fret = C blues scale
start point 10th fret = D blues scale

Blues scales are used as the foundation of many blues guitar solos.

Target time: down and back, 20-30 seconds

DATE:					
TIME:					

Top Tip
- fingertips
- pressing down
- just behind the fret

86

Extras lesson 2: Six must-know minor chords

A minor

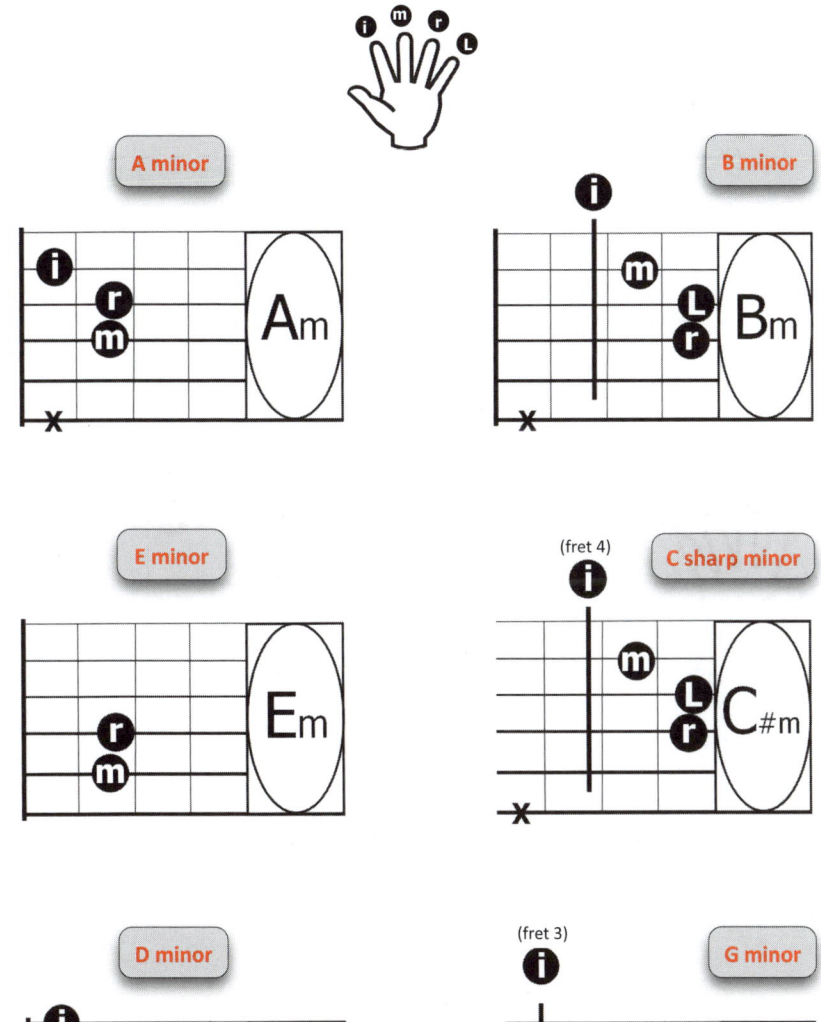

Am

B minor

Bm

E minor

Em

(fret 4)

C sharp minor

C#m

D minor

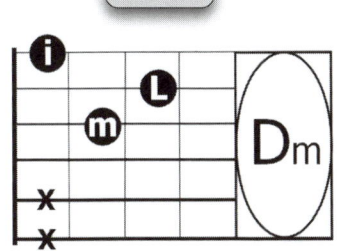

Dm

(fret 3)

G minor

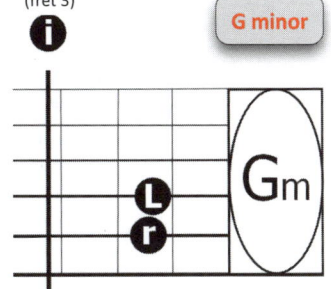

Gm

Extras lesson 3: Full-bar chord shapes

Don't be afraid of bar chords!
These are more about chord shapes that move up and down the fretboard. Bar chords give you great versatility by allowing you to take the same chord shape, and move it up and down the fretboard to make new chords.

With a bar chord your index finger presses down on multiple strings acting as a moveable nut or capo, while the middle, ring or little finger create the different chord shapes.
Remember to keep your index finger as straight as possible, budged up, right behind the fret.

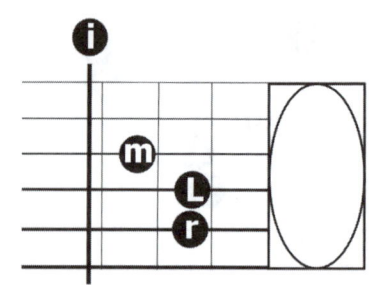

Full-bar major chord shape

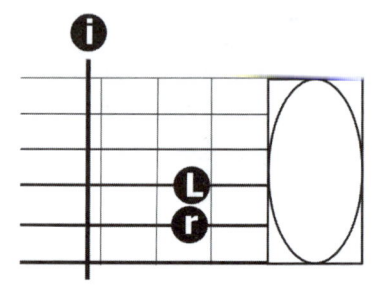

Full-bar minor chord shape

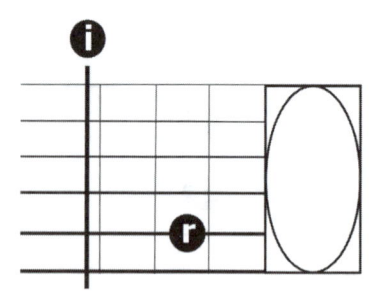

Full-bar minor 7th chord shape

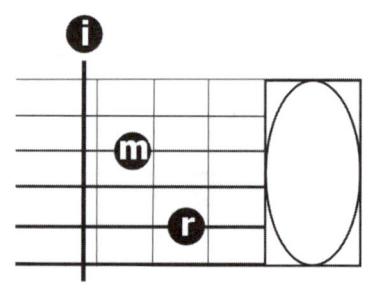

Full-bar 7th chord shape

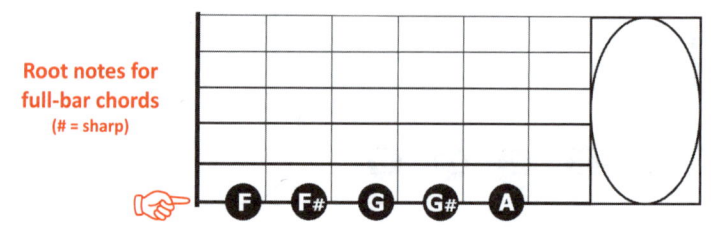

Root notes for full-bar chords
(# = sharp)

F F# G G# A

Root notes for the full-bar chords are on the 6th string.

Extras Ch6 E4

Extras lesson 4: Half-bar chord shapes (only using strings 1-5)

Remember the shapes for each type of full-bar and half-bar chord.
Starting from the root note will really help.
Like a tree, every chord is built up from the 'root' bass note.

Root notes for the half-bar chords are on the 5th string.
Root notes for the full-bar chords are on the 6th string.

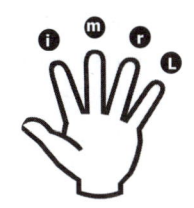

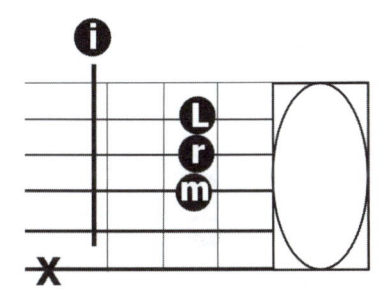

Half-bar major chord shape

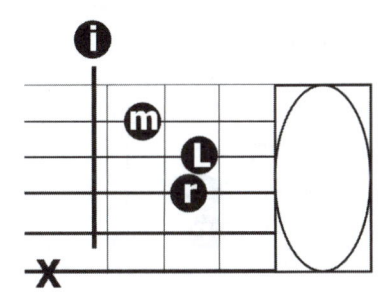

Half-bar minor chord shape

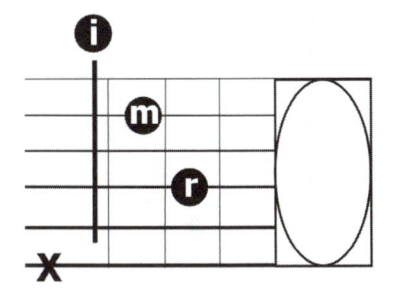

Half-bar minor 7th chord shape

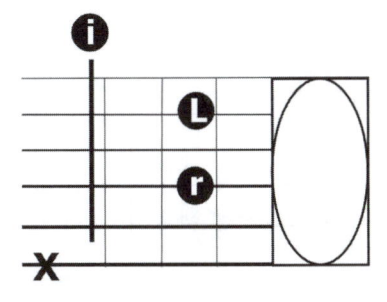

Half-bar 7th chord shape

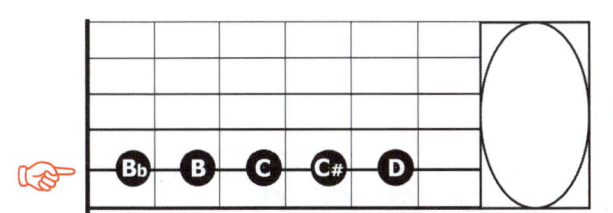

Root notes for half-bar chords
(b = flat
= sharp)

Bb B C C# D

Root notes for the half-bar chords are on the 5th string.

89

Extras lesson 5: Ten cool riffs

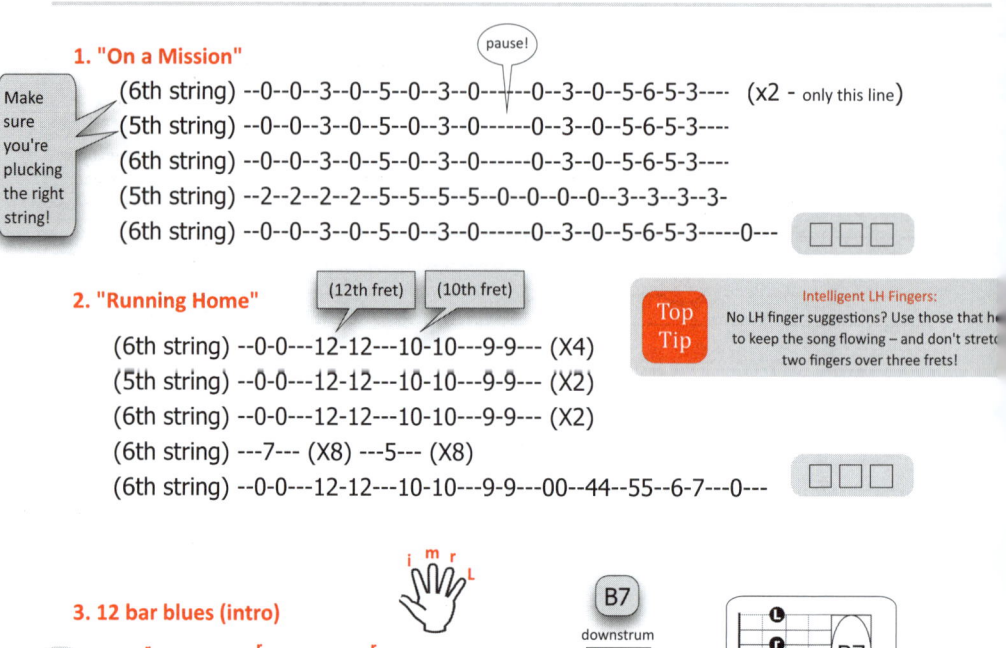

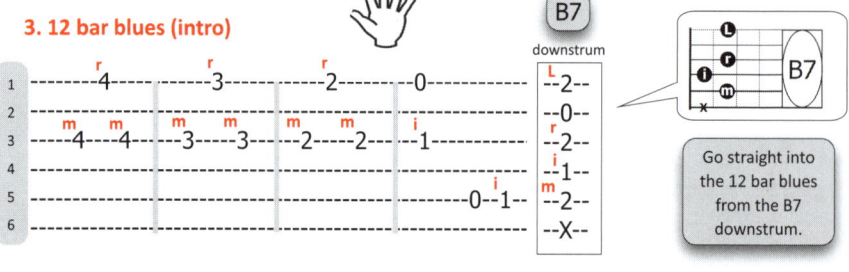

1. "On a Mission"

Make sure you're plucking the right string!

(pause!)

(6th string) --0--0--3--0--5--0--3--0-- | --0--3--0--5-6-5-3---- (x2 - only this line)
(5th string) --0--0--3--0--5--0--3--0------0--3--0--5-6-5-3----
(6th string) --0--0--3--0--5--0--3--0------0--3--0--5-6-5-3----
(5th string) --2--2--2--2--2--5--5--5--5--0--0--0--0--3--3--3--3-
(6th string) --0--0--3--0--5--0--3--0------0--3--0--5-6-5-3-----0---

2. "Running Home"

(12th fret) (10th fret)

Top Tip — Intelligent LH Fingers: No LH finger suggestions? Use those that he to keep the song flowing – and don't stretc two fingers over three frets!

(6th string) --0-0---12-12---10-10---9-9--- (X4)
(5th string) --0-0---12-12---10-10---9-9--- (X2)
(6th string) --0-0---12-12---10-10---9-9--- (X2)
(6th string) ---7--- (X8) ---5--- (X8)
(6th string) --0-0---12-12---10-10---9-9---00--44--55--6-7---0---

3. 12 bar blues (intro)

```
        r           r           r
1 ------4-------- ---3-------- ---2------- ---0-----------
2 ------------- ---------- ---------- ------------
   m   m     m   m     m   m     i
3 --4---4--- --3---3--- --2---2--- ---1--------
4 ------------- ---------- ---------- ------------
                                        i
5 ---------- ---------- ---------- ---0--1---
6 ---------- ---------- ---------- ------------
```

B7 downstrum
```
L
--2--
--0--
r
--2--
i
--1--
m
--2--
--X--
```

Go straight into the 12 bar blues from the B7 downstrum.

4. 12 bar blues (works well as a duet with 'Blues solo' on page 28)

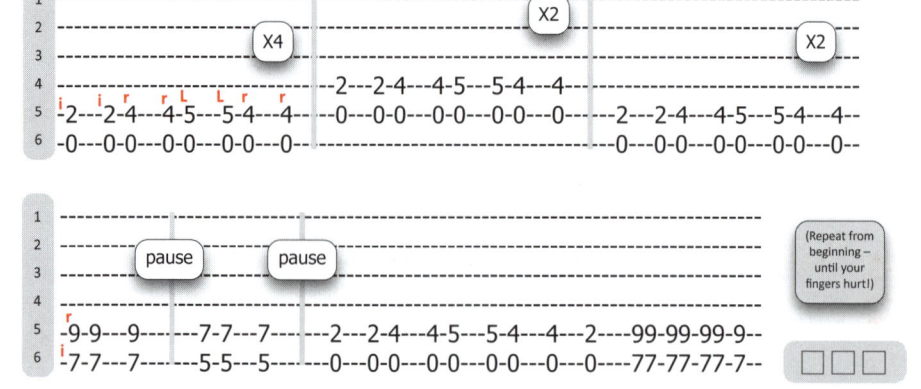

```
1 -------------------- ----------------------- X2 ---------------------
2 -------------------- ----------------------- ----------------------
3 ------------ X4 -------- ---------------------- ----------- X2 ---------
4 -------------------- --2---2-4---4-5---5-4---4--- ---------------------
   i   i r    r L   L r    r
5 -2---2-4---4-5---5-4---4--- --0---0-0---0-0---0-0---0--- --2---2-4---4-5---5-4---4---
6 -0---0-0---0-0---0-0---0--- -------------------- --0---0-0---0-0---0-0---0---
```

pause   pause

(Repeat from beginning – until your fingers hurt!)

```
1 --------------------
2 --------------------
3 --------------------
4 --------------------
   r
5 -9-9---9------7-7---7---- --2---2-4---4-5---5-4---4---2---99-99-99-9--
6 -7-7---7------5-5---5---- --0---0-0---0-0---0-0---0----77-77-77-7--
```

Extras Ch6 E5

5. "Setting Sun"

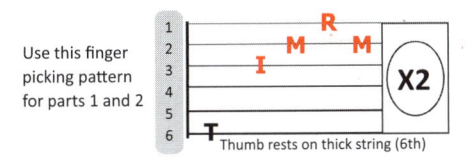

Use this finger picking pattern for parts 1 and 2

Thumb rests on thick string (6th)

Part 1

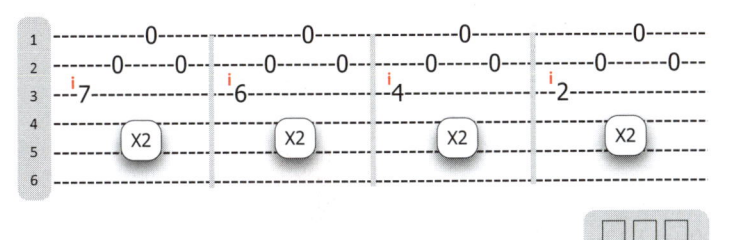

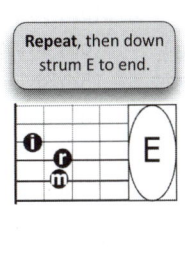

```
1 ----------0-------------0-------------0-------------0------
2 ---0------0-----0-------0-----0-------0-----0-------0------
3  i-7------      i--6----       i--4---       i--2---
4    X2             X2             X2             X2
```

Repeat, then down strum E to end.

E

Part 2

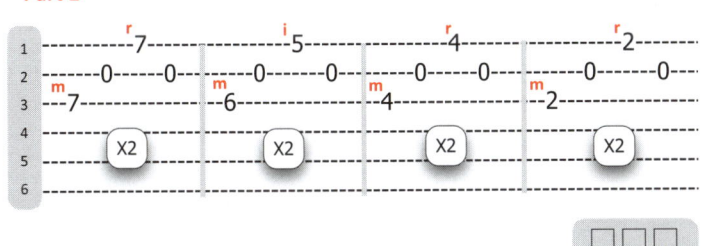

```
1 -----r-7-----------i-5-----------r-4-----------r-2------
2 ---0------0-------0------0-------0------0-------0------0--
3  m-7----         m--6---         m--4---         m--2---
4    X2             X2              X2              X2
```

Repeat, then down strum E to end.

Part 3 (Hold notes ringing for 4 beats each)

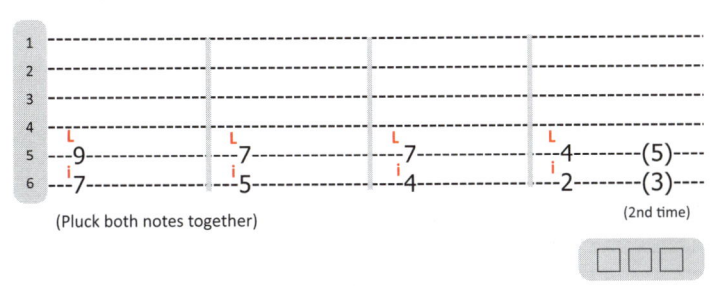

```
1 -----------------------------------------------------
2 -----------------------------------------------------
3 -----------------------------------------------------
4    L              L              L              L
5 ---9----------7----------7----------4--------(5)---
6 i-7---------i-5--------i-4--------i-2--------(3)---
```

(Pluck both notes together)   (2nd time)

Repeat, then down strum E to end.

"Setting Sun" also works well as a duet or trio.
Each part will sound good with any other, so feel free to experiment.

Top Tip In any song, how you end a piece is as important as how you play the piece; try slowing down as you near the end, and let the final chord or note ring for five seconds, gently dampening the strings with your right hand to finish.

6. "Soft Steps"

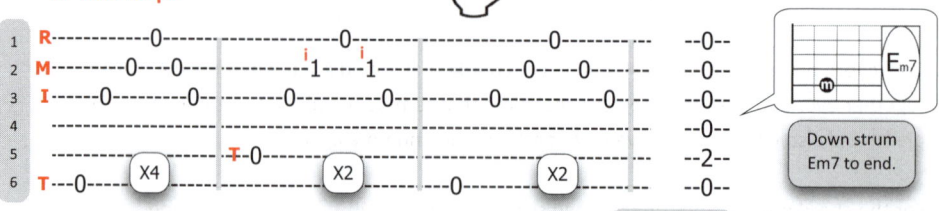

```
1  R------------0-------------------0-----------------0-----------  --0--
2  M--------0----0------------1-----1------------0-----0----------  --0--
3  I-----0----------0--------------------0--------------0---------  --0--
4  ----------------------------------------------------------------  --0--
5  ------------------------T-0-----------------------------------  --2--
6  T---0-------  X4  ----------  X2  --------------0---  X2  ----  --0--
```

Down strum Em7 to end.

7. "Runaway Train"

(12th fret)   (10th fret)

(6th string) --0-0---12-12---10-10---9-9-----0-0---4-4---5-5---6-7-- (X2)
(5th string) --0-0---12-12---10-10---9-9-----0-0---4-4---5-5---6-7--
(6th string) --0-0---12-12---10-10---9-9-----0-0---4-4---5-5---6-7--
(5th string) --2-2----6--6-----7--7-----8-9-----0-0---4-4---5-5---6-7--
(6th string) --0-0---12-12---10-10---9-9-----0-0---4-4---5-5---6-7----0----

8. "Blues Rock" 2's = index, 3's = middle

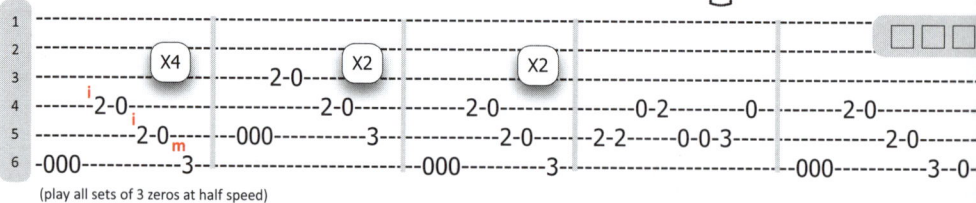

```
1 --------------------------------------------------------------------------
2 --------------------------------------------------------------------------
3 -------------X4-----------2-0---  X2  -------------  X2  -----------------
4 -------i2-0------------------2-0----------2-0-----------0-2------0-----2-0------
5 ----------2-0----------000-----------3----------2-0------2-2-----0-0-3-------2-0---
6 -000-----------3---------------------------------000--------3------------000----------3--0-
```

(play all sets of 3 zeros at half speed)

9. "Blues Bass" 2's = index, 4's = ring, repeat riff until smooth and play 0 to end

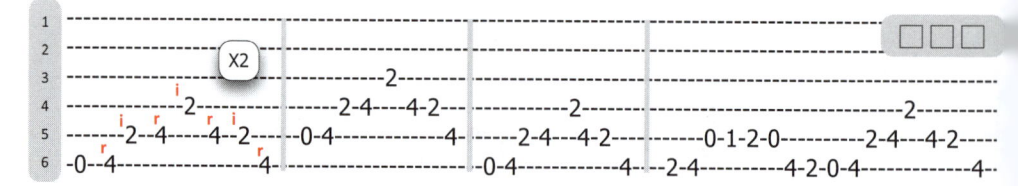

```
1 --------------------------------------------------------------------------
2 --------------------------------------------------------------------------
3 -----------X2-----------------2--------------------------------------------
4 ---------i2----------2-4---4-2-----------2-----------------------2---------
5 ---i2-4-r-r-i4-2------0-4--------4----2-4---4-2--------0-1-2-0----------2-4---4-2----
6 -0--4-----------r4----------------0-4----------4---2-4--------4-2-0-4-------4--
```

10. "Run for Cover"

(6th string) --0--0--12--0--10--0--9--7-----0--0--12--0--10--0--9--10- (X2)
(5th string) --0--0--12--0--10--0--9--7-----0--0--12--0--10--0--9--10-
(6th string) --0--0--12--0--10--0--9--7-----0--0--12--0--10--0--9--10-
(5th string) --2--2--6--6--7--7--8--9---------0--0--4--0--5--0--6--7-----
(6th string) --0--0--12--0--10--0--9--7-----0--0--4--0--5--0--6--7----- (--0-- to end)

Extras lesson 6: Ten cool chord progressions

Cool chord progressions are just a bunch of chords that sound great when they're played together over and over. It can be the chocolate that tempts people to the guitar in the first place, and also what players love to go back to time and time again.

For the chord progressions on this page strum each chord 1 2 and 3 and 4 and, or down strum each chord four times. (1234's = down strums, 'ands' = upstrums)

1. "E Quartet"

(TAB version)

```
1  --0----0----0----0----
2  --0----0----0----0----
3  --1----2----4----6----
4  --2----4----6----7----
5  --2----4----6----7----
6  --0----0----0----0----
```

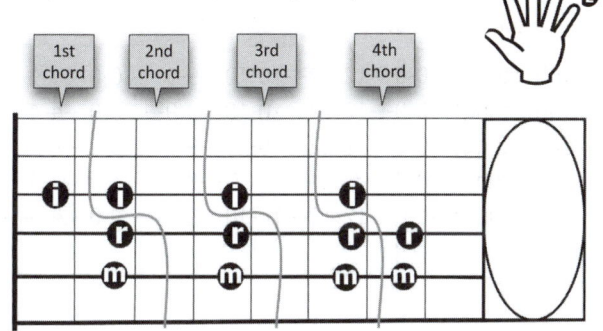

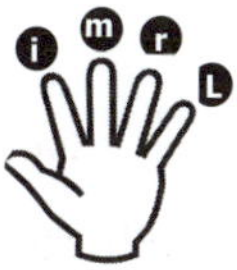

1st chord — 2nd chord — 3rd chord — 4th chord

2. G/D/Em7/C2

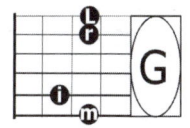

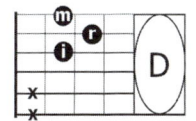

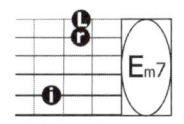

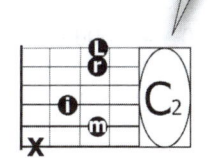

G — D — Em7 — C2 (Repeat until smooth)

(technically C2 is 'C add 9', but this book uses the shorthand equivalent)

3. "D prog"

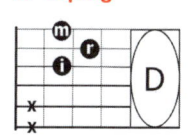

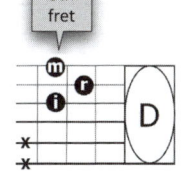

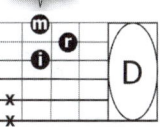

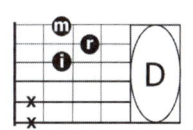

D — D (5th fret) — D (7th fret) — D (Repeat until smooth)

4. E/G/D/A

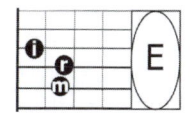

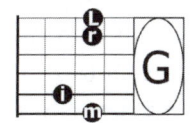

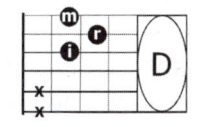

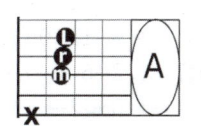

E — G — D — A (Repeat until smooth)

Ch6 E6 Extras

5. D/Em7/C2/G

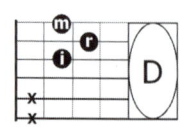

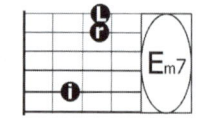

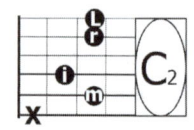

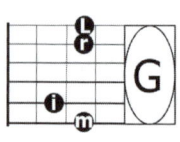

6. D/A/C2/G

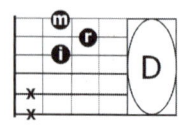

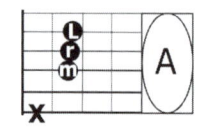

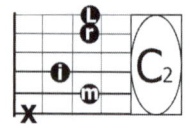

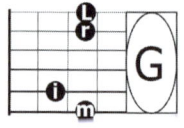

7. D/Bm/Em7/C2

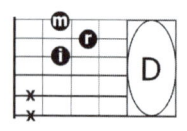

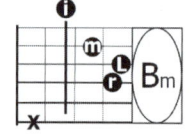

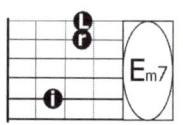

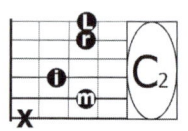

8: G/C2/Em7/D

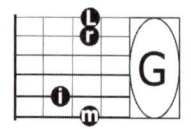

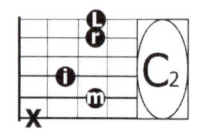

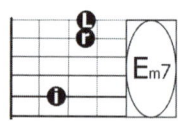

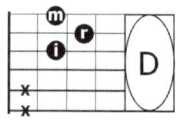

9. E/G/A/C

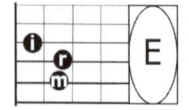

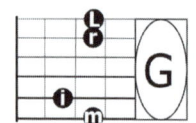

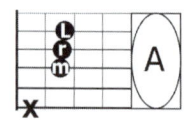

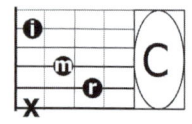

10. A/C#m/Bm/E

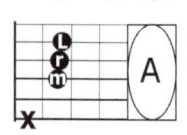

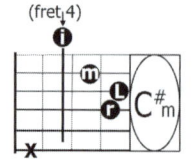

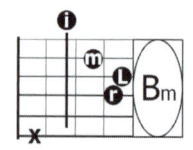

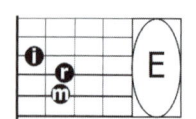

(fret 4)

Top Tip

As with all these chord progressions, feel free to experiment with your own rhythms and strumming patterns. Remember, there are no rules! The progressions above are merely a useful framework to do with what you feel: swap the chords around, spend longer on some chords than others, and don't forget that the greatest songs ever written often use the simplest of chord progressions repeated over and over.

Extras lesson 7: "Minuet in G" (Bach)

This is a short guitar intro to the much longer song by the famous German classical composer, written for the harpsichord.

I have suggested which left hand fingers to use as a helpful guide.

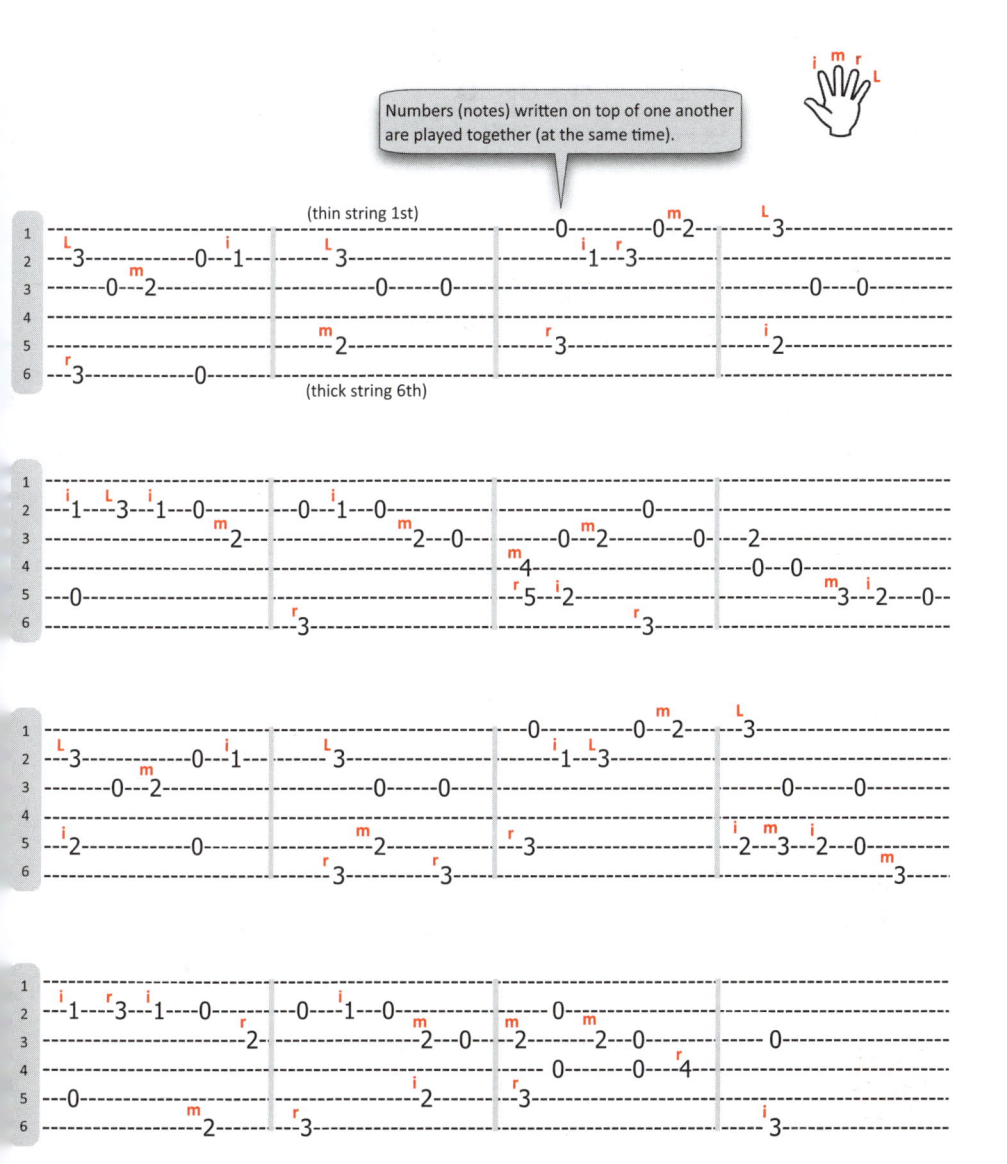

> Numbers (notes) written on top of one another are played together (at the same time).

```
                                                                    m        L
1 -----------------------------(thin string 1st)----------------0--------0--2-------3--------------
     L                  i              L                            i    r
2 ---3----------0---1-------------3-------------------------------1---3------------------------------
         m
3 -------0---2-----------------------------0------0-------------------------------0----0-----------
4 ------------------------------------------------------------------------------------------------
                                m                      r                        i
5 -----------------------------------2-----------------------3--------------------2---------------
     r
6 ---3----------0----------------(thick string 6th)---------------------------------------------
```

```
     i    L   i                  i                                      m       L
1 ---1---3---1---0---------0---1---0-------------------0------------0--2------3---------------
                                                                 i   L
2 ---------------------------------------------------1---3------------------------------------
                 m                  m                     m
3 ---------------2-----------------2---0------0---2---------0---2-----------------------------
                                         m
4 -----------------------------------4---------------------------0---0-------------------------
                                     r   i                                  m   i
5 ---0-------------------------------5---2--------r---3-------------3---2---0---------------
                 r                                                        r
6 ---------------3------------------------------3--------------------------------------------
```

```
                                                                    m        L
1 -----------------------------------------------------------0--------0--2-------3--------------
     L                  i              L                            i    L
2 ---3----------0---1-------------3-------------------------------1---3------------------------------
         m
3 -------0---2-----------------------------0------0-------------------------------0------0----------
4 ------------------------------------------------------------------------------------------------
     i                          m              r                     i    m    i
5 ---2----------0------------------2--------------3----------------2---3---2---0-------------
                                r              r                                   m
6 -------------------------------3---------------3---------------------------------3----------
```

```
     i    r   i                  i                      m   m
1 ---1---3---1---0---------0---1---0-------------0----------------------------------------
                 r                       m              2     2                  0
2 -------------------------2-------------2---0-------------0-------------0-------------
3 ---------------------------------------------------0---------0-----r-----------------
                                         i              r        4
4 ---0-----------------------------------2----------3--------------------------------
5 ---0-----------------------------------------------------------------------------------
                 m              r                                    i
6 ---------------2------------3--------------------------------------3-----------------
```

Extras lesson 8: "Greensleeves"

You can finger-pick this (**T, I, M, R, M, I** on each chord) or down strum each chord once. If down strumming, it might help by counting six beats between each chord.

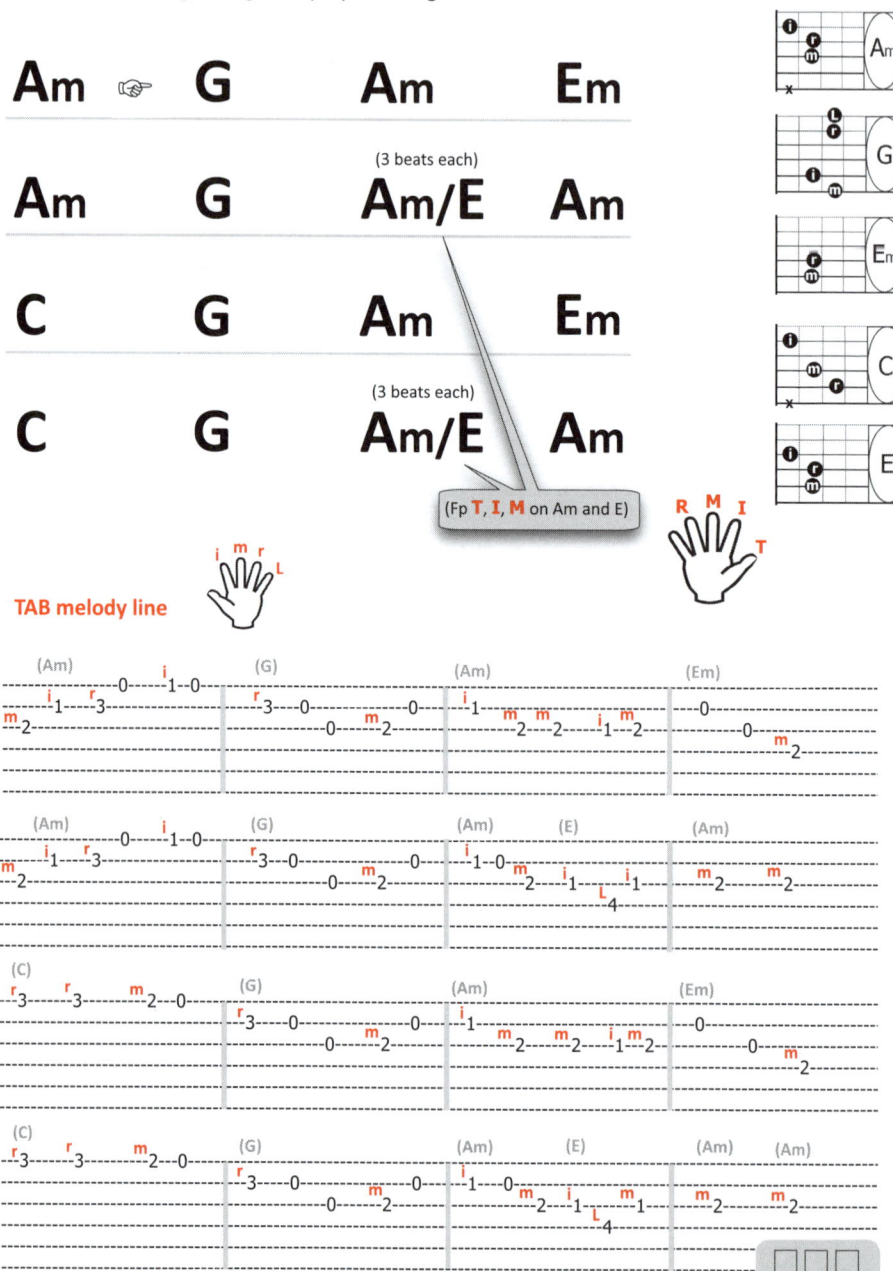

Am	☞	G	Am	Em
Am		G	(3 beats each) Am/E	Am
C		G	Am	Em
C		G	(3 beats each) Am/E	Am

(Fp **T, I, M** on Am and E)

TAB melody line

```
    (Am)                (G)              (Am)              (Em)
1 -----------0-----1-0--|--------------|--------------|----------------
2 ---i--1-r-3------------|-r-3---0------|-i-1---m-----i|m-0-------------
3 -m-2--------------------|-------0--m-2-|-------2---2-1--2|--------0--m----
4 -----------------------|--------------|--------------|-----2----------
5 -----------------------|--------------|--------------|----------------
6 -----------------------|--------------|--------------|----------------

    (Am)                (G)              (Am)      (E)      (Am)
   ----------0-----1-0---|--------------|-----i-----|----------|----
   -m-i-1-r-3-------------|-r-3---0------|-i-1-0-----|-m-      -m-
   -2---------------------|-------0--m-2-|-----m-2-1-L-i-1-    -2-      -2-
   -----------------------|--------------|------------4---|----|----

    (C)                 (G)              (Am)              (Em)
   -r-3----r-3---m-2--0--|-r-3---0------|-i-1---m---m--i-m-|--0-------
   -----------------------|-------0--m-2-|-----2---2-1--2---|------m-2-

    (C)                 (G)              (Am)     (E)      (Am)   (Am)
   -r-3----r-3---m-2--0--|-r-3---0------|-i-1-0-  m i  m    m       m
   -----------------------|-------0--m-2-|-----2-1-L-1-     -2-     -2-
                                                   4
```

Extras lesson 9: Ten easy songs (using the chords of D, G, and A)

1. "Jingle Bells"
2. "Happy Birthday"
3. "The Grand Old Duke"
4. "Oh When the Saints"
5. "Swing Low"
6. "Amazing Grace"
7. "Auld Lang Syne"
8. "Ten Green Bottles"
9. "Merry Christmas"
10. "He's Got the Whole World"

1. "Jingle Bells"

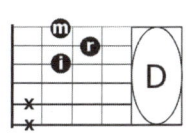

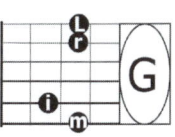

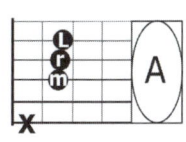

D   D   D   D
Jingle bells, jingle bells, jingle all the way,

G   D   A   A
Oh what fun it is to ride, on a one horse open sleigh, hey!

D   D   D   D
Jingle bells, jingle bells, jingle all the way,

G   D   A   D
Oh what fun it is to ride, on a one horse open sleigh.

2. "Happy Birthday"

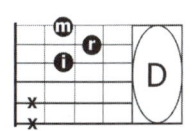

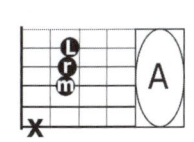

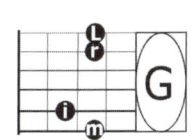

(D)
       D   D   D   A
Happy birthday to you,

A   A   A   D
Happy birthday to you,

D   D   D   D   G   G
Happy birthday dear (doo daa),

G   D   D   A   D
Happy birthday to you.

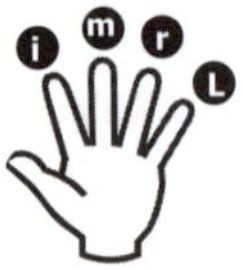

3. "The Grand Old Duke of York"

```
        D     D    D   D
Oh the grand old Duke of York,
     A       A      A    A
He had ten thousand men,
     D            D       G       G
He marched them up to the top of the hill,
        D           A    D
And he marched them down again.
        D         D          D   D
And when they were up, they were up,
     A         A            A   A
And when they were down, they were down,
     D         D  G     G
And when they were only half way up,
           D    A    D
They were neither up nor down.
```

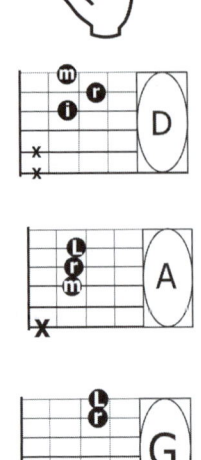

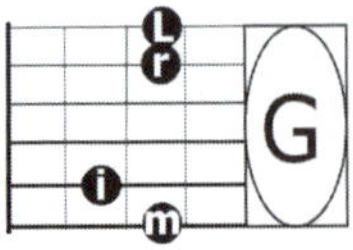

4. "Oh When the Saints"

```
           D   D
Oh when the saints,
        D   D
Go marching in,
           D    D    A  A
Oh when the saints go marching in,
        D D    G    G
I want to be in that number,
           D    A    D
Oh when the saints go marching in.
```

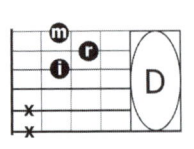

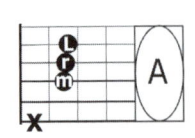

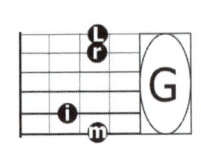

Extras Ch6 E9

5. "Swing Low"

```
        D   D      G  D
Swing low,    sweet chariot,
   D         D     A   A
Coming for to carry me home,
      D   D      G  D
Swing low,    sweet chariot,
   D         A     D   D
Coming for to carry me home.
     D        D      G    D
I looked over Jordan, and what did I see?
   D         D     A   A
Coming for to carry me home,
     D   D    G         D
A band of angels coming after me,
   D         A     G   D
Coming for to carry me home.
```

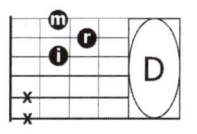

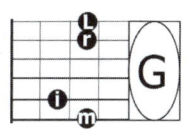

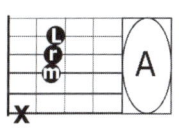

6. "Amazing Grace"

```
     D     D
Amazing grace,
        G      D
How sweet the sound,
       D     D    A   A
That saved a wretch like me.
     D    D
I once was lost,
     G    D
But now am found,
        D    A   G   D
Was blind, but now I see.
```

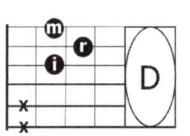

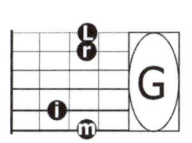

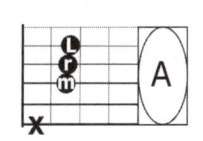

7. "Auld Lang Syne"

```
         D    D     A    A
Should auld acquaintance be forgot,
    D    D     G    G
And never brought to mind?
         D    D     A    A
Should auld acquaintance be forgot,
    G    G    D    D
For auld lang syne?
```

CHORUS:
```
    D    D    A       A
For auld lang syne, my dear,
    D    D    G    G
For auld lang syne,
         D    D    A    A
We'll take a cup of kindness yet,
    G    G    D
For auld lang syne!
```

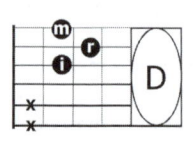

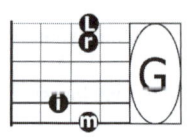

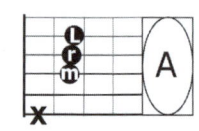

8. "Ten Green Bottles"

```
 D       D      A       D
Ten green bottles sitting on a wall,
 D       D      A       D
Ten green bottles sitting on a wall,
         G      D
And if one green bottle,
       A       G
Should accidently fall – there'll be...
```

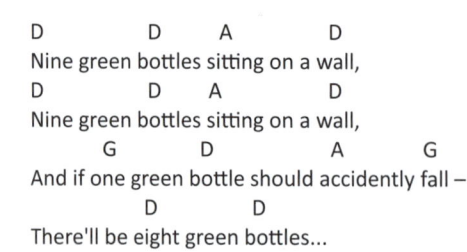

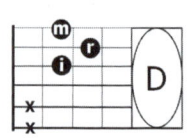

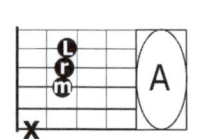

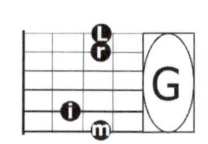

```
 D       D      A       D
Nine green bottles sitting on a wall,
 D       D      A       D
Nine green bottles sitting on a wall,
         G      D           A      G
And if one green bottle should accidently fall –
             D       D
There'll be eight green bottles...
```

Extras Ch6 E9

9. "Merry Christmas"

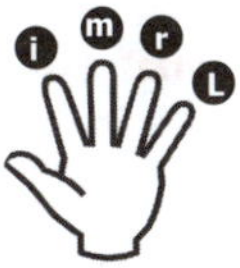

```
    D              G
We wish you a merry Christmas,
    G              A
We wish you a merry Christmas,
    D              G
We wish you a merry Christmas,
      G   (A)  D
And a happy new year.
    D           A
Good tidings we bring
    G           D
To you and your kin,
    D              A
We wish you a merry Christmas
      G   (A)  D
And a happy new year!
```

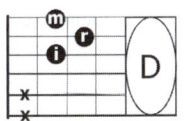

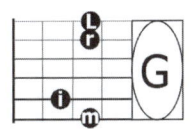

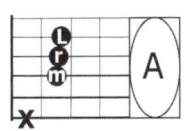

10. "He's Got The Whole World in His Hands"

```
            D  D  D    D
He's got the whole world in his hands,
            A  A  D    D
He's got the whole world in his hands,
            D  D  D    D
He's got the whole world in his hands,
            A     A    D
He's got the whole world in his hands.
```

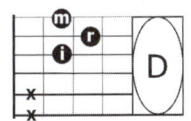

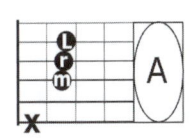

'Where are all the classic pop and rock songs?' – I would have loved to have included easy versions of famous songs, but copyright fees make it financially unviable! My own view is that if you can learn to play these (equally classic but not quite so trendy) songs, you'll be more confident having a go at the songs you do want to learn by downloading them from the many helpful websites on the internet.

Extras lesson 10: Really useful chord page

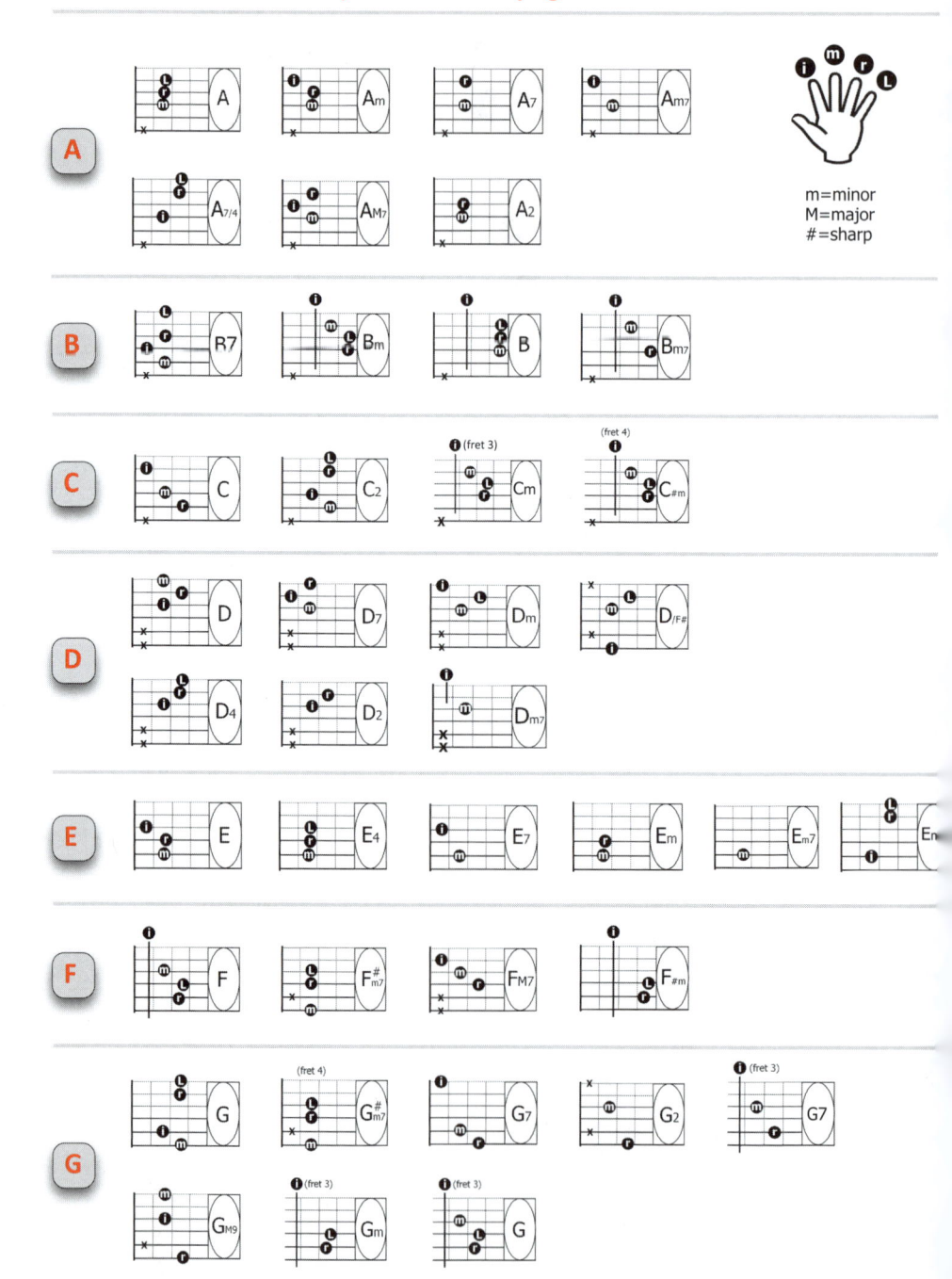

m = minor
M = major
# = sharp

A: A, Am, A7, Am7, A7/4, AM7, A2

B: B7, Bm, B, Bm7

C: C, C2, Cm (fret 3), C#m (fret 4)

D: D, D7, Dm, D/F#, D4, D2, Dm7

E: E, E4, E7, Em, Em7, En

F: F, F#m7, FM7, F#m

G: G, G#m7 (fret 4), G7, G2, G7 (fret 3), GM9, Gm (fret 3), G (fret 3)

Guitar Note Finder™

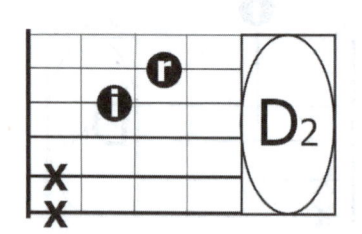

(my own)
Top 24 go-to chords

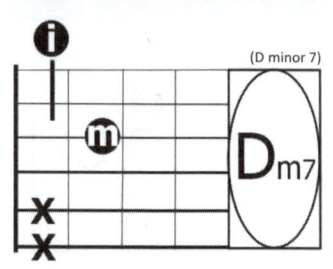

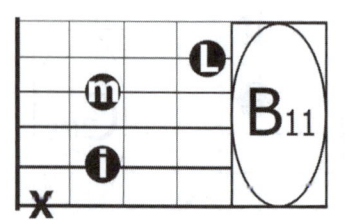

m = minor
M = major
# = sharp
X = don't play

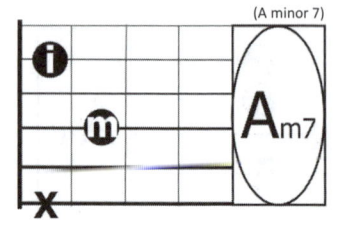

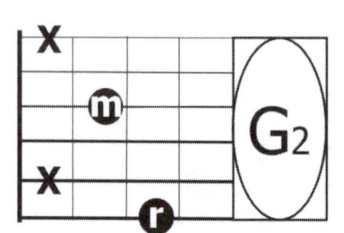

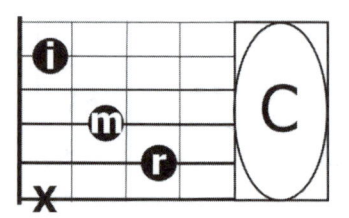

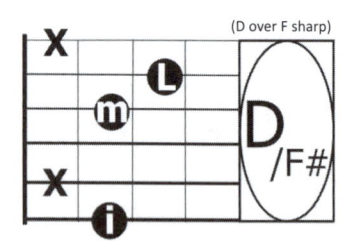

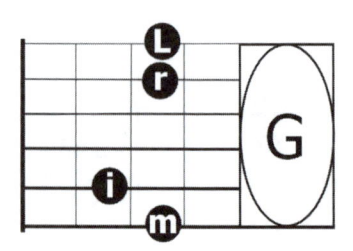

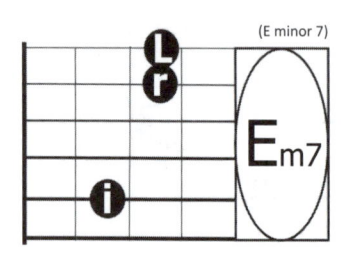

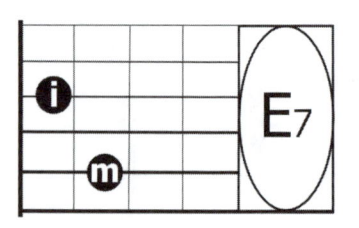

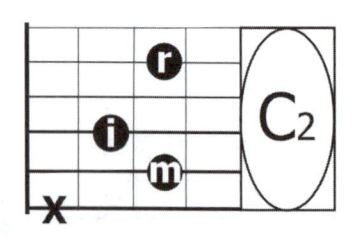

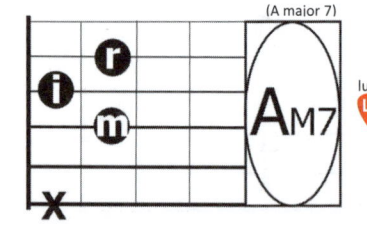

D2

Dm7 (D minor 7)

B11

Am7 (A minor 7)

G2

C

D/F# (D over F sharp)

G

Em7 (E minor 7)

E7

C2

AM7 (A major 7)

lush

105

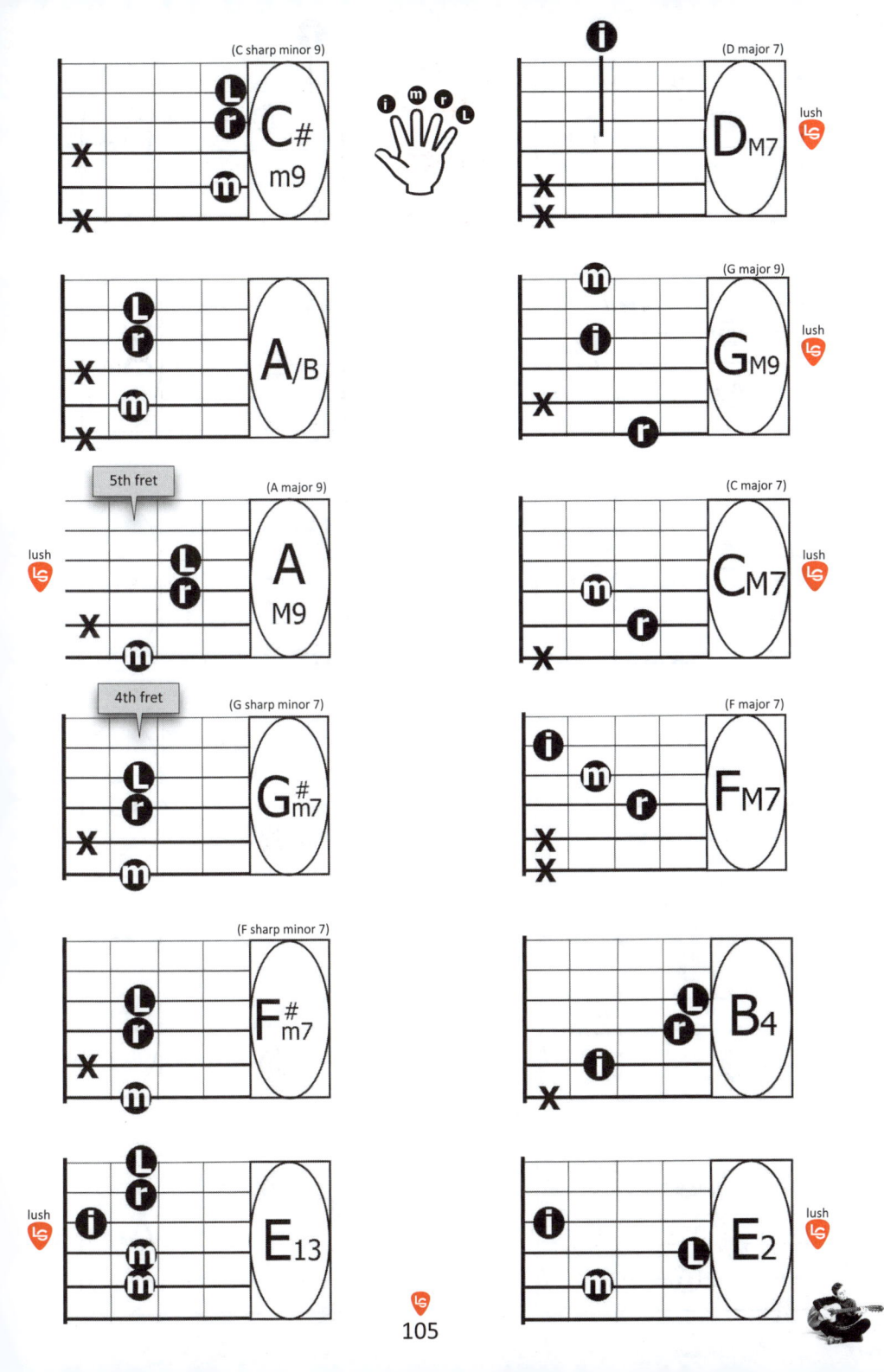

My own guitar journey started relatively late at 18. I had already been dabbling on the piano for nearly ten years and although failing grade 1 at eight years old, I just carried on playing and experimenting with new sounds and chord progressions. At 16 I started writing songs and singing live, but found a soft voice with a loud piano a bad mix. A couple of years later I was at a Ralph McTell concert and saw just him on stage with a guitar and thought to myself, *now that's what I want to do*. I was so impressed with how someone could play really well and not even need to look at their fingers on the fretboard! He was able to put his heart and soul into his songs and didn't need the clutter of a band. It was the whole deal right there on that stage; the voice as the **melody**, the chords as the **harmony**, and the strumming as the **rhythm**. This is why watching a performance that encapsulates the three most powerful elements of music is so mesmerising.

So I knew where I wanted to be, but I just had to work out how to get there.
I knew a guy who played a bit, and he showed me a few chords. To begin with I just needed a simple progression, a few chords that sounded cool when played together. Once I found them, the frustration of pausing for every chord change (while I adjusted my fingers on the fretboard) motivated me to repeat and repeat and repeat until the chord changes sounded smooth and even. I had the FF scales and the full-bar chord exercise (down strumming F shape X8 from fret one through seven and back) and the "E quartet" (p94), and so I just played these until I got fed up with them. I realised I had to master this piece of wood and strings and knew that repetition would be the key; 'do something enough times and the fingers get the message!'.

I probably spent 30 minutes to an hour playing four or five times a week for a month until I noticed dramatic results. Because it's you yourself working on it, sometimes it's not apparent until you try a familiar chord sequence and suddenly realise you can play it through smoothly and evenly this time.

There were weeks of soreness on the fingertips, and (especially with bar chords) a real muscle ache between the thumb and index finger, but it soon disappeared. Progress was in definite stages; I would feel I was developing really quickly for a month or two and then I seemed to plateau, but then have a burst of improvement once again. I think the key was that I kept at it. Even for the busy times I made sure I practiced for at least 15 minutes, three or four times a week.

I hope this book has helped to inspire you to pick up the guitar and learn some tunes. We all have different amounts of time to spend, but if we are as consistent as we can be, our fingers will learn what to do in time, and we'll be amazed at how much we can achieve.

For questions, comments, or queries please feel free to get in touch! It's good for me to constantly review and refine so that this method is more understandable and helpful for others.

Andy

andy@loveguitar.co.uk

This is Nicholas. He's been playing for over a year now and really enjoys playing simple tunes over and over. He loves the guitar because when he plays it relaxes him. He wants to be in a band one day.

This is Fred. He's been playing for well over a year (ok, 50 years), and started learning so he could accompany 'sing alongs' at his local church. At 90 he still gets up at 6.30am every morning and practices for an hour towards his Grade 1.

This is Jemimah. She grew up with guitars all round the house and has been playing ever since she could hold one. She downloads chord charts of her favourite songs and loves singing while she strums. She now teaches others to play.

This is Ben. He started playing at 14 when he started a band and dressed up like a rock star in his garage. He still wants to be a rock star, but until then he loves to noodle a few times a week trying out new combinations of notes and chords.

This is Andre. He picked up the guitar at nine when his older brother started playing. At 17 he started writing and singing his own songs. He really appreciates being able to just pick it up and play in a style that suits his mood.

This is Helen. She's been playing since she was 17 and started learning so she could accompany her voice, and also lead worship at her local church. She loves singing and this gave her the motivation to learn to play well.

This is Jason. He's been playing since he was eight, and started after a few friends wanted to learn as well. It took a few weeks until he felt he was improving, and now he loves being able to pick it up and play regardless of how he's feeling.

This is Dave. He's been playing for over 30 years and started to learn because he liked a girl who was also learning. Within a month he'd learnt three songs, and within six he was in a band. Within a year he'd married the girl.

This is Jane. She's been playing for over 25 years now and has managed to learn the chord of C. She can play it quite well. The next chord she wants to learn is G. There is no way she wants to be in a band.

This is Will. He's been playing for 3 years and he loves it because it makes him happy. He thinks it's an easy instrument to play if you practice, and great to be able to learn new fun songs. One day he wants to be in a band with his mates.

Index

"Amazing Grace", 99
"Auld Lang Syne", 28, 100
"Ball Around Bee", 74
"Blues Rock", 92
"Blues Bass", 92
"Blues Solo Bass", 27, 28
"Blues Solo", 27, 28
"C in 5", 80
"Call from Space", 73
"D Prog", 93
"E Against B", 67
"E Quartet", 93
"E Squeeze" riff, the treat! 31
"Easy Peasy", 21
"Feel the Beat 2", 64
"Feel the Beat", 64
"G in 5", 80
"Give Me Oil in My Lamp", 27, 29
"God Rest", 30
"Going to Sleep", 69
"Grand Old Duke of York", 26, 98
"Greensleeves", 96
"Happy Birthday", 22, 23, 25, 97
"He's Got The Whole World", 101
"High and Low", 71
"In and Out", 65
"It's the Police!", 77
"Jingle Bells", 22, 24, 97
"Lazy Gee", 71
"Lift Off", 21
"Low Lazy Gee", 71
"Merry Christmas", 23, 25, 29, 101
"Minuet in G", 95
"Oh When the Saints", 23, 25, 98
"Old MacDonald", 22,
"On a Mission", 90
"Runaway Train", 92
"Run for Cover", 92
"Running Home", 90
"Saints Away", 76
"Setting Sun", 91
"Skimming Stones", 72
"Small Steps", 75
"Soft Steps", 92

"Swing Low", 24, 99
"Ten Green Bottles" 21, 24, 26,100
"The B Song", 67
"The E Song", 67
"The G Song", 68
"Three in a Boat", 68
"Two in a Boat", 68
"Up and Down", 65
"Waking Up", 69
"Yankee Doodle", 30
12 bar blues, 90
16 Chord Block, 42/43, 44
16 Chord Block (strumming), 45
24 go-to chords, 104/5
Back of the book extras, 83
Bar line, 66
Beats Per Minute (BPM), 63
Blues scale, 86
Blues scale in G, 26
Bridge, 6
C major scale, 78
Chord box, 9, 34
Chord of A, 39
Chord of A minor, 89
Chord of B minor, 89
Chord of B7, 40
Chord of C# minor, 89
Chord of D, 41
Chord of D minor, 89
Chord of E, 38
Chord of E minor, 89
Chord of Easy A, 36
Chord of Easy B7, 37
Chord of Easy E, 35
Chord of G minor, 89
Chords debrief, 46
Classical notation, 60
Classical notation debrief, 82
Contents, 3
Crotchet, 63
Dotted minim, 70
Double bar line, 66
FF scales, 84
Finger names, 7

Finger picking, 13, 47
Finger picking 16 CB, 56/7
Finger picking debrief, 60
Finger picking styles, 59
Frets/Fretboard, 6
Full-bar chord shapes, 88
G major scale, 30, 79, 85
Guitar note finder, 81, 103
Guitar parts, 6
Half-bar chord shapes, 89
How to finger pick, 47
How to play chords, 33
Index, er, this page!
Introduction, 2
Left hand home position, 8
Major scale, 85
My own 24 go-to chords, 104/5
Minim, 64
Notation, 60
Note tails, 66
Nut, 6
Open string names, 7
Position dots, 6
Really useful chord page, 102
Rest stroke, 12
Right hand home position, 9
Scales, 78, 84
Semibreve, 70
Six must-know chords, 10
Six must-know minor chords, 87
Sound hole, 6
Stave, 66
Strumming, 14, 45
TAB, 11, 19
TAB debrief, 32
Tempo, 63
Ten cool chord progressions, 93
Ten easy songs, 97
Ten cool riffs, 90
The ten basics, 5
Time signature, 66
Treble clef, 66
Tuning, 16
Tuning pegs, 6